PLEASURE PRINCIPLES

Politics,
Sexuality
and Ethics

Edited by Victoria Harwood
David Oswell
Kay Parkinson
and Anna Ward

LAWRENCE & WISHART
LONDON

Lawrence & Wishart Limited
144a Old South Lambeth Road
LONDON SW8 1XX

First published 1993

Photoset in North Wales by
Derek Doyle & Associates, Mold, Clwyd
Printed and bound in Great Britain by
Biddles Ltd, Guildford

PLEASURE
PRINCIPLES

Contents

Contents

Preface

But what is it I really like? What is it that I really want, sexually? Why is it that I turn away from him even though I feel pleasure and rising lust? I do know what I imagine when I masturbate. Yet my innermost sexual fantasies, with their emphasis on passivity and total male dominance are frightening, because they are so contradictory to what I, as a feminist, think.[1]

This mixture of rules and openness has the effect of intensifying sexual relations by introducing a perpetual novelty, a perpetual tension and a perpetual uncertainty which the simple consummation of the act lacks. The idea is also to make use of every part of the body as a sexual instrument.[2]

Helen Thorning's quote above shows just one aspect of the difficulties of ethically living our sexuality, namely how our desire may not marry up with how we feel it 'ought' to be; and how our fantasy may not fit our practice. The 'ought' can be particularly strong because it is not the ought of societal norms but the freely chosen ought of a political position which we would defend with all our hearts and minds. This collection starts from the assumption that the terrain of sexuality is fraught with complexities. How we negotiate them politically is its subject. The title, *Pleasure Principles: Politics, Sexuality and Ethics* can only give a flavour of the issues discussed. The chapters do not make up a check list of ethically 'right' positions but instead form an exploration, from diverse perspectives, of what it means to be politically sexual or sexually political.

The 80s and 90s have seen an ever increasing proliferation of books on sexuality. These are primarily written from an academic, medical or 'how-to' perspective. We wanted to produce something which seriously addresses a politics of pleasure without losing either the politics or the pleasure.

As soon as the word politics is attached to the term pleasure it is not possible to think further without considering the allied areas of power and identity. *Power* because pleasure and sexuality are not innocent activities which come from nowhere and are unproblematically experienced in an unmediated, timeless fashion but rather are part and parcel of the world of late twentieth century capitalism and its heterosexist institutions. *Identity* because how we experience pleasure and our sexuality is intimately bound up in who we feel we are, how and where we live and where we come from.

Body Politic/Erotic Selves

We are not alone in trying to articulate the ethics of a political sexuality. This book emerged from a conference, *Body Politic/Erotic Self*, held in London in July 1991. The organisers, ourselves included, decided that we wanted to put together a conference on the broad theme of sexuality and in particular the future of sexual politics in the 1990s. This desire was in part due to our recognition of an increasing feeling of unease with the moralistic sexual and gender politics of the 70s and 80s. This unease had registered both at an academic level and, more importantly perhaps, at the popular level of people's everyday lives. As part of the process of deciding what topics to cover we sent our questionnaires to people 'in the field' asking what they felt were the issues which should be addressed. It was at the conference itself that the recurring theme of an ethical sexuality recurred, with its attendant emphasis on power and identity. We decided to gather up some of the threads spun by this enthusiastic gathering to begin to catalogue an emerging engagement with a politics of sexual pleasures.

The contributions in this collection, and the discussions at the conference, showed an understanding of the term power which contains all its manifestations from the micro level of pillow talk to the macro level of the economic muscle of the porn industry or the legislative power of the state. These extremes are still traditionally seen as part of different terrains. Personal behaviour is still felt to be the area where ethics operate whilst politics is about 'larger' issues. For this reason we felt that talk of an ethics of pleasure is appropriate in its recognition of the small decisions and dilemmas of the everyday negotiation of sexuality whilst a politics of pleasure can address both activism and the formation of an analysis of how societal currents in all their forms participate in the 'doing' of sexuality. Principles are individually inflected but have collective resonance.

A Politics of Identification

Identity politics are undoubtably in a time of change. Whilst we acknowledge our debt to the empowering sexual politics of the 70s and 80s which allowed us to proudly identify ourselves as black, as lesbian, as gay, as woman, we have increasingly seen a desire to move beyond its dogmatisms which fix such identities in a 'natural' and limiting mould. We have attempted to use emotional points of investment and identifications within communities of experience, or ways of living, as less rigid ways of looking at sexual 'identity'.

We took as our starting point 'the personal is the political' but we wanted to look at how the personal was inflected with the contradictions of the political rather than as that which must be defined by the political. In the earlier political moment we see the private being dictated by the public and the individual subsumed within the collective. However, instead of opting for a privatised individualism, as so often voiced by the sexual libertarians of both the Right and the Left, we wanted to look at how our individual lives are shaped by an increasingly contradictory and fragmented terrain in which our personal politics cannot be governed by an over-arching moral code.

It is in this sense that the book makes connections with a wider set of debates about the question of value in this postmodern age. How do we govern our sexual conduct given this diversity and the crumbling of our hallowed traditions?

We have gathered together a number of voices which we hope return a sexual politics to the hybridity of everyday practices and understand that a politics of the sexual needs to grasp the tension between the diversity of our everyday sexual pleasures and the social formation of relations of power. We cannot merely 'correct' our sexual conduct from a reading of the forms of domination.

Pleasure Principles

Likewise we cannot divorce sexuality from the domains of power. There is always a space in-between which is messier and more hybrid, but which in many ways is more inspiring and pleasurable.

'Pleasure Principles' are central to an exploration of feminist and gay and lesbian politics and also to the politics of AIDS. A new language and ethics of sexuality has begun to surface in which it is possible to think sexy and dirty, to think and act out difference without forfeiting political correctness. We see this collection as part of the forging of that new language, a language which tries to get to grips with the complexities of our everyday sexual existence whilst encompassing a theory and politics which is neither predefined nor prescriptive.

We have not attempted to, indeed could not, be definitive. What we have tried to do is raise a whole range of issues in a thoughtful way without sacrificing accessibility. The issues of sexual ethics are not confined to academic circles. We did not exclude academic contributions, as a glance at the list of contributions shows, but we felt that activists and artists were also tackling issues of sexual ethics, often in more interesting ways. We invited contributions from censors and anti censors, film-makers and cultural critics, photographers and poets.

Additionally we felt that a variety of forms, rather than a series of 'authoritative' essays, aided this process of dialogue. We have made a magazine of images and words with different styles of presentation; photos, essays, journalistic articles and poems.

In the midst of all these words, images and theory it is easy to forget that sexuality has a more carnal element. *Coito ergo sum.* The safe sex material has been deliberately positioned to enclose the whole. Theory cannot be divorced from practice. Similarly the list of organisations at the end will hopefully make more of you *make your sexual practices your political activities.*

Rather than presenting a single linear argument the chapters are intended to be read in any order. However, whilst the reader is invited to pick and mix, the contributions illuminate each other as they address a number of overlapping themes. Issues which recur are pornography, censorship, sexual practice and mores and the 'right' sexual behaviour, reformulating identity politics, defining and producing sexy images, and, of course, AIDS.

Preface

Broadly speaking, the contributions focus on one of two areas. First they deal with sexual representation, particularly visual representation. Second, the contributions are concerned with intervention in the public arena whether through activism or regulation. The two areas, of representation and intervention, are not discrete. For example, producing AIDS posters is obviously bound up with issues of representation as well as activism. Similarly the film censor regulates on the basis of his/her understanding of how representation works.

Some of the contributions address the boundaries which define the ethics of pleasure, for example in the debates around pornography and censorship. What the contributors do not address is the strictly unpleasurable, the darker sides of sexuality where displays of power are more blatant, for example child abuse or rape. We do not intend to belittle their importance by this omission. However, as we have said earlier this collection is not definitive. Its focus is on pleasure, since we felt that this is an area in which the Left, in Britain, the States and elsewhere, has been notoriously weak.

The Pleasure Principle

As we outlined above, the contributors come from many backgrounds. They are activists, legislators, artists, lovers. As such they use many different approaches from grass-roots to high theory. We would just like to nod in the direction of the latter by highlighting the final reason for our choice of the title *Pleasure Principles*. Although the book never directly engages with psychoanalytic theory, it is evident that many of the contributions come out of an implicit engagement with this significant body of theory. It is in this sense that our title *explicitly* pays our dues to Freud. Post-Freudian psychoanalytic theory has been enormously productive for film theory and an understanding of visual pleasure; for feminism with its analyses of the constitution of the female subject and its emphasis on sexual difference and for gay and lesbian analyses and politics in its polymorphously perverse groundings.

But it can also be restrictive. For example, film theory's emphasis on the male oedipal gaze as the source of visual pleasure has provided a useful critique of gender relations within contemporary society but it forecloses women from taking up the position of the subject of the look. By utilising the concept of a politics of difference it is possible to build a more diverse architecture of looks; gay and straight voyeurs, men looking at men, women looking at men, women looking at women, men taking the position of the feminine gaze. Several of the contributors try and articulate this new political space. This space recognises diversity, recognises the radical instabilities of such definitions as gay or straight, yet still retains a political thrust. In such a space it is still possible to shout 'that is unjust.' Whether they refer to this space as that of the Joke (Sue Golding), or of hybridity (Isaac Julien) or as Jeffrey Weeks does as the 'politics of difference and diversity' they all recognise its importance. We hope, in part, this collection contributes to forming a language for that space.

The search for a new language of sexuality within the field of vision is a theme which is present in the contributions by Della Grace, Naomi Salaman, Sean Nixon and Isaac Julien. Della Grace in her photographs provides an ethnography of queer looks and desires. As a photographer she rejects the position of the voyeur at a distance looking down on her subjects. Naomi Salaman, in her photographs and essay, looks at a particular object of sexual pleasure in relation to a particular regime of representation. In her photographs she takes a witty view of our desire for the penis and takes various phallic substitutions from everyday life and imposes them onto the very infrastructure of our bodies. In her article she describes her aesthetic practice by looking at the question; what is pornography for women? In what sense can we talk about men as sex objects?

Both Sean Nixon and Isaac Julien raise questions about looking, masculinity and sexual identity. Sean Nixon considers the pleasures of men looking at men's bodies. He talks about the pleasures of men reading men's magazines, like *Arena* and *GQ*. He argues that while these magazines draw upon a reservoir of gay iconography, they do not position a gay male gaze alone, rather the reader is positioned within a set of looks which are both highly narcissistic and deeply ambivalent. It is out of this tension that so much pleasure is derived from looking at stylised bodies of men. In the interview with Isaac

Julien this ambivalence is discussed in relation to other questions about race and ethnicity. He talks about his own experiences as a 'young soul boy' and shows how the soul and disco clubs of the late 70s provided a hybrid space in which black and white, middle class and working class, and gay and straight could mix on the dance floor. The concern with the hybrid has been central to Isaac Julien's film-making. He talks about how his aesthetic/political practice attempts to break down the rigid hierarchy between high and popular culture and about how Queer cinema offers new representational strategies for a new sexual politics.

Acting

Anna Marie Smith, in her essay 'Outlaws as Legislators', talks about her work with the feminist anti-censorship group, PUSSY (Perverts Undermining State ScrutinY). She talks about the way in which lesbians and gays have taken up the hegemonic 'reproduction of state-like institutions within our own communities'. She argues that it is important to recognise ourselves as both legislators and outlaws.

The opening and the closing chapters consider contemporary discourses on sexuality within the context of HIV and AIDS. Jeffrey Weeks in 'An Unfinished Revolution' provides us with a history of the discourses on sexuality in the 20th century. He outlines the increasing liberalization and secularization of sex and talks about the difficulty of finding a language and an ethics of sexuality in this postmodern era. He finally shows us how 'the uncertainties and ambiguities that are shaping sexual mores at the end of this century' are dramatised in the HIV/AIDS crisis. Roberta McGrath looks at the discourses on sexuality in health educational AIDS/HIV material and frames her argument within a set of questions about power and resistance.

Quotidian Pleasures

Our everyday sexual lives are not limited to the bedroom. Our sense of our sexual selves spreads across our daily lives: fucking, looking, reading, dancing, watching films, dressing and so on. Jackie Kay in her poems writes about desire and sexual imagination. Her poems deliver a sense of what might be called sexual melancholy. Desire is always never satisfied. There are always other lovers and other relationships which both get in the way of, and yet also provide the threads for, the rich tapestry of passion described in her poems.

Ken MacKinnon in his essay 'Gays the Word – Or is it?', reiterates certain problems about the categorization of the sexual, but he frames this within a more fundamental problem about the binary opposition between heterosexuality and homosexuality. He looks at the question of bisexuality. Drawing upon his own personal memories as a Scottish school boy, fascinated with the sexual pleasures of the cinema, he questions the way in which our sexuality is disciplined and points to an ambivalence at the heart of our sexual identities.

Whilst the cinema can open up many sexual pleasures, it is also important, Geoffrey Wood argues, to consider the dangers of certain visual pleasures. He argues that the film censor's role is primarily to classify rather than to cut or ban. He makes a case for the role of a censorship body within a wider set of questions about power and regulation. He argues that sexual representations should not be left to be regulated either by the market, in which profit takes precedent over ethics, or the law, which is both heavy handed and less liberal than the British Board of Film Classification.

Avedon Carol is more circumspect about the usefulness of censorship. She focusses on the question of the sexual ethics of the self. She looks at the sexual pleasures of pornography and places this within a wider set of perverse activities. She argues that instead of proposing certain injunctions against the peverse, more sexual practices need to be governed by an ethics of sexual pleasures and perversities in which the freedom to talk about pornography or S/M, for example, and the freedom to pursue these activities, does not prescribe engaging in those activities. In this sense she argues that an opening up of the sexual to a diversity of pleasures must be accompanied by the progressive government of the self: the freedom to say 'No'.

Sue Golding, in her essay 'Sexual Manners' takes us on a theoretical romp through Wittgenstein via an entertaining S/M encounter. She laces this event together with a series of questions about sexual conduct, truth and the ethical formation of the self. And she closes with her description of an 'impossible place', a place which is beginning to take place. A place that has 'something to do with the cry: 'Freedom' … '. The place of the Joke.

> … the Joke is neither real nor unreal; it is invention, whose meaning erupts through its style; contoured and shaped by its technique, always tossing and turning and erupting and demolishing within the play of the game. Indeed, with the Joke, we get into more serious matters: a side-stepping of identity politics without losing an identity: a side-stepping of confession, ie, of having to 'confess' at every turn who it is we 'really' are, without losing the right to yell and kick and scream and be, well, inconsistent. To be able to … play the game which involves pleasure, and creativity, and fiction, and imagination and spectacle and beauty in all its sublime corrosiveness, false eyelashes, leather and decay – in short, a 'that' which involves a certain kind of courage, I suppose, a courage to refuse the Profound, and exchange it, mixed metaphors and all, for the surface of the risk.[3]

Victoria Harwood, David Oswell, Kay Parkinson and Anna Ward.

Notes

[1] Thorning, Helen, 'The Mother-Daughter Relationship and Sexual Ambivalence', *Heresies* vol 3 no 2 1981 p.3.
[2] From an interview with Michel Foucault conducted and translated by James O'Higgins in *Politics, Philosophy, Culture*, Lawrence D. Kritzman, Routledge, London 1988.
[3] Golding, Sue, 'Sexual Manners' in *Pleasure Principles* p.87, Harwood et al, Lawrence & Wishart, London, 1993.

Acknowledgements

No book is complete without a huge thanks to the many characters in the shadows providing inspiration, encouragement and hard graft. A special thanks goes to those dedicated few who helped to create the conference which was the initial inspiration for this collection. Thanks to the *Body Politic, Erotic Self* team – Joe, Kay, Mark, Marika, Davina, Sarah, Michael, Chip and Alex. Thanks to the contributors for their commitment and patience, and to Matt and Lindsay at Lawrence & Wishart. For their moral support and professional advice, thanks to Jean, Austin, Ed and Robin. And on a more personal note, for insightful comment, domestic tolerance, and simply 'putting up with us', we would like to say thanks to Nell, Bernadette, Eve, June, Alex, John, Angus, Vera, Robert, Roger, Wendy, Matt, Julian, Charles, Lisa and Luke.

And of course thanks to everybody else, too many to name, who contributed to the process of discovering Pleasure Principles.

An Unfinished Revolution: Sexuality in the 20th Century

JEFFREY WEEKS

What do we mean when we write about 'sexuality'? Sexuality pervades the air we breathe, but we still lack a common language for speaking about it. It is a topic which we can all say something about, and on which we are all in one way or another 'experts', but that, somehow, increases rather than decreases our confusions: sexuality, it seems, has so many 'truths' that we are left with a cacophony of noise, and precious little good sense. There has been an ever expanding explosion of discourse around sexuality in the past century, and the volume seems unlikely to diminish in the near future. Yet it is a subject which arouses the greatest anxieties and controversies, and increasingly has become a front-line of divisive political controversy and moral debate.

This is because the sexual touches on so many disparate areas of individual and social existence. When we think of sexuality we think of a number of things. We think of reproduction, which has traditionally been seen as the main justification of sexual activity, and with which western cultures at least have historically been most preoccupied. We think of relationships, of which marriage is the socially sanctioned, but far from being the only, form. We think of erotic activities and of fantasy, of intimacy and warmth, of love and pleasure. We relate it to our sense of self and to our collective belongings, to identity, personal and political. But we also think of sin and danger, violence and disease.

Nothing is straightforward when we try to think or speak of

1

sexuality. It is both the most private and personal of activities, and the most public. We still often speak of it in whispers, while it is all the time shouting at us from bill-boards, newspapers, radio and television, pulpits, the streets. Our own voices compete with, or may even be, those of priests and politicians, medics and militants, and all too many, many more.

So anyone rash enough to try to analyse its social forms, or predict what shape the kaleidoscope will next take, is treading on very dangerous ice. There are so many conflicting elements at play. For sex, despite its immediacy, is very much a cultural and a historical phenomenon. Whatever we like to think, we are not entirely free agents in this matter, any more than we are of anything else. Our choices are real and important, but they are also constrained by a very long and complex history and intricate power relations, which tell us, amongst other things, what is natural or unnatural, good or bad, permissible or impermissible. If there is a 'crisis of sexuality' today, it is because many of the fixed points which we think we need to guide us through the maze have been pulled down or obscured; and because the language of sexuality is muddied by a long and often painful history.

If there is a confusion about values and attitudes, that should not surprise us, nor should we imagine it is anything unique to us. We can find in the history of the past two hundred years or so almost all the themes that preoccupy us now, and similar laments about the decline of morals and a confusion of values.[1] Two hundred years ago, in the wake of the French Revolution, one of the formative moments of modern Europe, we find middle-class evangelists worried about the state of morality in Britain: they saw, or believed they saw, a dissolute, amoral aristocracy, a feckless, overbreeding working class. Surely, these moralists felt, we would end up like the French, drowned in chaos and blood, unless we all learned the importance of 'respectability', what became 'Victorian values'.

Some of the implications of these Victorian values became clearer a generation later as the poverty and disease of the new industrial towns began to confront policy makers. Just as today some conservative commentators seek to blame social ills on the existence of one parent families, so in the 1840s and 50s individual behaviour was blamed for what were transparently social ills. The result was a

2

renewed effort to moralise the masses into the image of their masters, an effort which by and large failed. The mores of the working classes may have been different from those of the middle class, but, as historians are now discovering, they were no less 'moral'.

Then take sex-related disease. Today our experience of sex is shadowed by the HIV/AIDS epidemic. In the nineteenth century the most feared scourge was syphilis, and we can find in the response to this, ominous pre-echoes of our modern reaction. In the 1860s a series of measures, the Contagious Diseases Acts, sought to control the spread of syphilis by enforcing compulsory examinations of those who were suspected of being prostitutes. The model for the acts were allegedly measures to control cattle. The result was inevitable: the intimidation of large numbers of women, growing hostility to state regulation, a radical movement of resistance, and no obvious impact on the incidence of the disease. Many of the more extreme measures proposed in the 1980s to control the spread of HIV – compulsory testing, detention of those suspected of spreading the disease – were prefigured a hundred years before.

As another example, let's take sexual abuse of children. Today we worry rightly about child sex abuse. But sexual abuse of children was raised in the 1830s in the context of debates about the impact of children working in the factories and mines; in the 1870s, in the report, no less, of the Prince of Wales's Royal Commission on Housing, in the context of housing overcrowding and the danger of incest; and in the 1880s, as a result of the panic about the 'white slave trade', when the age of consent for girls was raised eventually from 13 to 16. It takes different forms at different times, but abuse of children is not a new discovery, any more than our confusions and hesitations in confronting it are new.

The history of birth control reveals a similar pattern. Although the roots of the birth control movement are many and various, and its practice in many forms is probably as old as sexuality, its preoccupations over the past 100 years have been remarkably constant: how to balance the need for social regulation of the population with the rights of parents and of individual women to control their own fertility. When the National Birth Control Council, the immediate predecessor of the Family Planning

Association, was set up in 1930 it brought together a number of groups, some of which were deeply shaped by eugenicist ideas, preoccupied with the planned breeding of the best. One of the great fears of the time was that as the population declined, so the balance of the population would shift to those who were least 'fit' to bear the burdens of modern life. Today we are more concerned with the threat of overpopulation in the Third World, or of the implications of artificial insemination or extra-uterine conception, but the same anxieties and fears still intrude: we worry about who should breed, and under what conditions and whose control, as much as why. We do not like apparently the idea of sexuality being uncontrolled and unplanned, a matter of choice rather than social obligation.

Finally, there's the question of sexual identity. It is easy for us today to assume that the sexual categories and identities we work within, pre-eminently those of heterosexual and homosexual, are fixed and eternal, corresponding to essential differences transmitted (who knows how?) from the dawn of time. It is now clear, however, that these distinctions were only formulated in a recognisably modern form in the closing years of the nineteenth century, the result of a complex process whereby the norm of heterosexuality was established and reinforced by the drawing of boundaries between it and its dangerous other, homosexuality. This in turn was intricately related to the reformulation of gender relations, so that sexual and gender identities were locked together: manhood, in particular, was defined by refusing the temptation of homosexuality. The developments of the current century have made possible the emergence of strong and vibrant lesbian and gay identities that have challenged the heterosexual norm, just as social change and the rise of contemporary feminism have undermined the hierarchies of gender, but the point that I want to underline is that the nineteenth century, like the present, was haunted by the spectre of homosexuality. There is a nice historical symmetry in the fact that just over a hundred years after the Criminal Law Amendment Act of 1885 made all forms of male homosexuality illegal, the 'promotion of homosexuality' by local authorities was banned (through what became known as 'Clause 28'). Circumstances change, and so do laws; but a fear of homosexuality apparently remains.[2]

We can, in other words, see in the fairly recent history of

sexuality, many problems, dilemmas and anxieties remarkably similar to our own. They revolve essentially around boundaries, between men and women, adults and children, 'normal' and 'perverse' sexuality, between orthodox and unorthodox lifestyles and identities, between health and disease. I offer these examples not to suggest that nothing ever changes; on the contrary, I hope to show that there have been profound changes in attitudes towards sexuality. My intention, rather, is to warn against that facile history which looks back to a 'golden age' when somehow everything was better, more fixed and certain, than it is today. It wasn't, and we are not going to be able to deal with the challenges of the close of this century if we seek a return to the largely mythical, supposedly wholesome values of the last.

Nostalgia for a golden age of order and harmony is one danger when thinking of sexuality. There is another temptation as we approach the end of the millennium, to identify with that sense of an ending which seems to characterize the closing of a century, to reconstruct a *fin de siècle* mood which sees the uncertainty of our own age of anxiety as being the same as that of the most famous *fin* of all, that of the late nineteenth century. Rather than regretting a better past, this mood wallows in the 'sexual anarchy' which some contemporary commentators saw as characterizing the ending of the last century.[3] This in turn fits into a postmodern consciousness which in its most deconstructive mood celebrates the impossibility of a master, legitimizing discourse for sexuality, glories in heterogeneity, the return of the repressed of sexuality, the *bouleversement* of all values, and the subversive power of the perverse.

This opens up challenging perspectives for thinking about sexuality anew. This is especially the case as a new scholarship undermines the dominant myths and meanings that emerged in the late nineteenth century.[4] As hallowed traditions crumble, we are being forced to raise questions of value: by what criteria, and by whose sanction, can we say that this activity, desire, style, way of life, is better or worse, more or less ethically valid, than any other. If the Gods are dead, or dying, or the secular myths of History and Science lie discredited before us, is anything permitted? Postmodernist writing has been effective in tearing apart for scrutiny and critique many of our taken-for-granted beliefs. It has been less effective in elaborating alternative values. I shall return to this issue later.

I want now to look at certain key trends which seem to me to underlie the changes we have experienced over the past century, and whose consequences look set to dominate the 1990s. I identify these as, first, the secularisation of sex, an inadequate term which does, nonetheless, pinpoint some key changes; second, a liberalisation of attitudes, which has reshaped both the law and social attitudes; and third, the challenge of diversity, perhaps the key change to which everything else is secondary. Finally, I want to look at the future of all three in the context of the current crisis around HIV disease and AIDS. I am not going to offer predictions, because nothing is predictable in the world of sexuality; nor do I wish to suggest a blueprint for a new ethics: blueprints are what have so often led us astray. But I shall try to offer a framework for understanding what too often seems like a meaningless flux.

The Secularisation of Sex

First of all let's look at what I am calling the secularisation of sex. By this I mean the progressive detachment of sexual values from religious values – even for many of the religious. This has a long history, but perhaps the key feature was the process, beginning in the mid nineteenth century, whereby the initiative for judging sexuality passed from the churches to the agents of social and mental hygiene, primarily in the medical profession. Science promised to prop up, or replace, religion in explaining or legitimizing sexual behaviour. Already by the end of the century, some feminist and other critics were arguing that doctors were the new priesthood, imposing their new (overwhelmingly masculine) imperatives on the bodies of women. Since then, the arbiters of sexual values have tended to be increasingly doctors, sexologists, psychologists, social workers, even politicians, rather than priests.

This is, of course, an unfinished revolution, as all those who have campaigned for birth control, sex education, the rights of sexual minorities or the right of sexual choice know very well. You can still be labelled as both immoral and sick, sinful and diseased, all at the same time, if you offend the norms. Nor have the churches of various kinds given up the struggle. It is only a few years since the British Chief Rabbi welcomed the 'swinging of the pendulum' back to traditional values (though as I have suggested, that tradition was itself pretty confused).[5] Elsewhere in the world, as well as in this country, we have seen what W.H. Auden called the 'fashionable madmen' attempting to assert the links between religious fundamentalism and a particular (restricted) type of sexual behaviour, and these attitudes have had many local successes to their credit. The Republican Party convention in the USA in 1992, to quote just one recent example, managed to impose on the party an extremely conservative moral agenda; opposing abortion, campaigning against the recognition of homosexual rights and affirming the merits of 'family values'.[6]

Yet it seems that despite all the huffing and puffing, the anguished debates and the like, the process of secularisation has gone too far to reverse fundamentally, as the spectacular electoral failure of the Republicans in 1992 suggests. Even in the most traditional of churches, such as the Roman Catholic, perhaps the majority of the faithful (and a significant minority of its own priesthood, apparently) ignore the Pope's injunctions against birth control, and in the USA we see openly gay Catholic priests and lesbian nuns. The fevered efforts of religious traditionalists to turn back the tide testifies, I would argue, as much to the success of secularisation as to the power of religion.

But at the same time as the power of religion is undermined, so the claims of a scientific morality have been subverted. The early sexologists, men (usually men) such as Richard von Krafft-Ebing, Havelock Ellis, Magnus Hirschfeld, even Freud, believed that what they were doing was to put the laws of sexuality onto a scientific basis, to provide a rational basis for sex reform: 'through science to justice', proclaimed Hirschfeld in Germany before his library and legacy were piled on the Nazi book-burning pyre.[7] Today we are a little more sceptical of the claims of science to guide us through the moral maze. Many of those labelled and categorized by the early science of sex (women as the 'dark continent', homosexuals as a biological aberration) have resisted the labels, and developed their own definitions in a sort of grass roots sexology which plays with and subverts inherited descriptions.

7

Pleasure Principles

The significance of all this is profound, because what it does is to take responsibility for sexual behaviour away from external sources of authority and to place it squarely on to the individual. This introduces into the debate on sexuality a contingency that is, for many, troubling and enfeebling. But it is important to recognise that this sense of contingency is not just confined to the domain of sexuality. On the contrary, the existence of a dual consciousness, of the necessity, but difficulty and pain, of individual choice, can be seen as a key element of our late modern sense of self. As the 'juggernaut of modernity', in Anthony Gidden's phrase, gathers momentum, dissolving all certainties and transforming all fixed identities and relationships, so the sense of the contingency of self, its provisional placing in a changing world, a narrative quest for partial unity rather than a fixed attribute of essential being, becomes paramount.[8] In the twentieth century the Enlightenment belief in the constitutive individual, Man (and it was usually male) as the measure of all things, has been severely challenged: by Freud's discovery of the dynamic unconscious, by the recognition of cultural and sexual diversity, by the challenges of feminism and lesbian and gay politics, by the historical and deconstructive turns in the social sciences, by the experiences of fragmentation which for many characterizes late or post-modernity. In all these contexts sexuality becomes problematized, dethroned from its position of being a determining essence. Yet at the same time, as if by a necessary reflex, sexuality becomes a source of meaning, of social and political placing, and of individual sense of self.

This of course poses many problems, and is probably the main focus of anxiety about sexuality today. The public debates about sexuality since the 1960s, including those around the so-called 'permissive reforms' of the law on abortion, homosexuality, divorce, censorship and birth control, far from being a licence to do what you want, were actually about finding the right balance between private pleasures and public policy, between freedom and regulation. In other ways, the rise of the caring professions, the pressure on organisations like Relate (the National Marriage Guidance Council), and the proliferation of experts and therapies of various sorts, indicate the difficulties of relying on ourselves alone. But the conclusion we must draw from this secularisation seems to me

8

inescapable: today we see sexual matters as essentially about individual choice. The debate is about the legitimate limits of choice, not about the legitimacy of choice itself.

Liberalisation of Attitudes

This is closely related to the second trend I have identified, the growing liberalisation of attitudes over the past generation. By this I mean the gradual abandonment of authoritarian or absolutist values, and a growing stress on individual decision-taking about sexuality. People are generally more accepting today of birth control, abortion, pre-marital sex, co-habitation before or instead of marriage, divorce, and homosexuality than ever they were in that supposed haven of the 'sexual revolution', the 1960s. And despite its espousal of Victorian values, and a certain closing of space around a number of key issues, this liberalisation continued to grow, perhaps even increase during the Thatcher years, and is likely to continue during the 1990s.[9]

Here are a few examples. About 50 per cent of single women lived with a man before marriage by the end of the 1980s, compared to 7 per cent in 1970, and over triple the figure when Mrs Thatcher took office in 1979. The proportion of children born outside marriage rose from 12 per cent in 1980 to 25 per cent in 1988. For women under 20, the figure is much higher: around 82 per cent in the north-west and north of England. Britain now has one of the highest divorce rates in Europe, over 150,000 a year in the 1980s, and 4 out of 10 marriages, it is projected, will end in divorce in the 1990s.[10]

Then there is the touchstone issue of abortion, a highly contested issue throughout much of the west (it was, for example, one of the issues that threatened to hold up German unification in 1990, because of the conservative fear in west Germany of the liberal laws in the east), and a highly divisive issue in the USA. Despite strenuous efforts since the law was liberalised in Britain in the 1960s to reduce the time during which termination is permitted, all have failed, not only because a majority of MPs were resistant or because of the campaigns of pressure groups, for example, the National Abortion Campaign, but because access to abortion had become the wish of the majority of the population. I am sure that abortion will

9

continue to be a key moral issue, but it is difficult to believe that there will be a consensus in Britain in the near future for restrictive change.

These examples suggest to me that there has been a crucial long-term shift in the way we see sexual activity and relationships. I would be cautious about calling it a revolution. In many ways it is startlingly like a reversion to much earlier, pre-'Victorian values' mores, with a high rate of formal illegitimacy, toleration of certain forms of pre-marital sex, and a relatively late age of marriage. This is accompanied, however, by a new explicitness in talking about sex which magnifies and dramatises the impact of the transformations that have taken place.

There is, however, an ambiguity in this continuing liberalisation, which underlines the limits of the changes that have taken place, and this is seen most clearly in relation to homosexuality. According to opinion surveys, there was a continuing liberalisation in attitudes towards homosexuality from the late 1960s into the early 1980s, then a shuddering set back, which has only recently, according to the survey *British Social Attitudes*, been partially reversed. So while in 1983, 62 per cent censured homosexual relationships, by 1987, in the wake of the AIDS panic, this had risen to 74 per cent of those interviewed. Public hostility was even sharper when asked their attitudes to lesbians and gay men having the right to adopt children. In 1987, 86 per cent would forbid lesbians adopting children, and 93 per cent gay men. A Gallup Poll shortly after the Clause 28 controversy in late 1987, early 1988, confirmed a deep seated hostility: 60 per cent thought that homosexuality should not be considered an accepted lifestyle, compared with 34 per cent who did approve – though perhaps significantly for the coming decade, 50 per cent of those under 35 were accepting.[11] What seems to be happening is a greater acceptance of the fact of homosexuality ('live and let live') whilst there remains an ingrained refusal to see it as of equal validity with heterosexuality.

There is a sharp paradox in attitudes towards homosexuality. While prosecutions for 'homosexual offences' reached a height in the late 1980s only previously attained in 1954, before legislation, suggesting an increased police interest in the issue, while the popular press pursued people suspected of homosexual tendencies fervently, and while the incidence of 'queer-bashing' increased dramatically, there were abundant signs of a more general growth of the homosexual community. Social facilities continued to expand, gay characters appeared in soap operas on television, people spoke more easily about homosexuality than ever before. The prosecutions, 'queer-bashings', and Clause 28 can be seen as distorted responses to real changes taking place in attitudes to non-heterosexual behaviour. It is not too much of an exaggeration to say that Mrs Thatcher, despite her rhetoric and actions, presided over the biggest expansion of the lesbian and gay community in its history.

This is in line with the wider point I am making: there seems to be a long-term shift both in beliefs and behaviours taking place which governments have only a limited power to effect. They can toughen laws, pursue errant fathers, condemn the 'promotion of homosexuality' and the like. They can contribute to the sum total of human misery. But they cannot force people to behave in ways that they don't want to.

This is, in part at least, recognized in the new legal framework that reached its apogee in the liberal reforms of the 1960s, but which still, if inadequately, shapes legal responses. The liberalization of the legal framework that followed the Wolfenden report on homosexuality and prostitution in 1957 signalled an abandonment of legal absolutism, that is a view of the law which saw it as embodying the moral norms of society. Instead, the new approach relied on a clear distinction between the role of the law, to uphold generally acceptable standards of public behaviour, and the domain of morals, increasingly seen as a matter of private choice (the 'Wolfenden strategy').[12] In practice this meant allowing, in the famous phrase, 'consenting adults in private' to pursue their personal ends without interference so long as the public were not unduly frightened. The actual implementation of the new legal framework was less clear cut, however. For example, abortion on demand was tempered by the need for medical authorization of abortions. The rights of homosexuals was restricted by narrow interpretations of 'consent' (which could be given only by those over 21, not at all in Scotland or Northern Ireland until a decade later, and never in the armed forces), and of 'privacy' (which was not recognized if more than two people were present, or potentially present). Regulation was changed, but not abandoned; the locus of control shifted. A form of sexual pluralism was recognized, but it was not fully legitimized. Yet it provided a space which has allowed sexual autonomy to grow. During the 1970s and 1980s there were various challenges to this legal compromise, especially with regard to pornography; but despite a harsher climate and a closing of space for social experimentation, the framework held, even under a political regime committed to moral conservatism. Clause 28 is again a test case. Although its intention was restrictive and punitive, it was still clearly within the framework of the Wolfenden strategy. It did not propose making homosexuality illegal, intending instead to prevent 'promotion'. Of course, by doing that, the government's intervention gave unprecedented publicity to homosexuality, and helped to forge a stronger sense of identity and community amongst lesbians and gay men than ever before.[13] But that is one of the paradoxes of legal involvement in sexual lives. The unintended consequences are often more important than the intended. The liberal legal experiment attempted as much to regulate as to free individuals, but its consequences have been to institutionalize a form of tolerance of diversity and choice. That tolerance falls far short of full acceptance of difference, as the case of homosexuality underlines. Nevertheless, it highlights my central point: legal and moral absolutism are fading as the guidelines of policy, but the alternatives have still to be fully worked out.

To close this discussion of what I have called liberalisation, I want to pin-point two further historic shifts that underlie some of the patterns I have mentioned. The first is the changing balance of relations between men and women. This is most obvious in the taken-for-granted assumption today that women have their own sexual needs and desires, with as much claim to satisfying them as men. This has been a long revolution since the nineteenth century, and one that is not clear cut or unproblematic. Some feminist historians have suggested that what has happened is a sexualisation of the female body on male terms, and for the servicing of men. Against this it is important to remember the struggles of women themselves for sexual autonomy and freedom of choice.[14]

Beyond this is a more profound questioning of the power relations between women and men, the result both of feminism and the changing role of women in the economy and society. Despite ups and downs in the path to full equality, there is no doubt that this represents a radical transformation of relationships, whose effects in the next decade are impossible to underestimate. We have already seen its impact in, amongst other things, the changing agenda on rape and sexual violence and a new concern with the sexual abuse of children, in all of which questions of power are to the fore.

The second shift that must be recognised is the growing recognition of the fact of sexual diversity. I have mentioned homosexuality, and the contradictory responses it evokes. But it is clear today that there is a much greater variety of beliefs, identities and relationships than our moral codes allow. The truth is that people's sexual needs and desires do not fit easily into the neat categories and moral systems we build to describe and contain them.

Both these shifts are critical elements in the third major trend I want to outline: the challenge of diversity.

The Challenge of Diversity

The heart of the challenge is this: we increasingly have to accept the fact of diversity. We know that people have different needs and desires, that they live in different types of households and have various sorts of relationships. But we are reluctant to accept the norm of diversity: that is, we still seek to judge people as if there were a common moral standard by which they should live. I believe that one of the key issues of the 1990s will be precisely the attempt to move from recognition to normalisation of diversity.

The constant laments about the impact of permissiveness and the evocation of 'Victorian values' during the 1980s suggested that the key changes we have noted – the rise of illegitimacy, the rising divorce figures, the new presence of homosexuality, etc. – indicated a drastic decline of moral standards, a disintegration of old values, leading to a threat to the very existence of the family. Interestingly, more recently, there has been a dawning recognition that something else is afoot: not so much a collapse of morals, as a change in their form, not so much a decline of the family, as the rise of different sorts of families. Angela Rumbold, when briefly the minister for the family in the late 1980s, suggested that these facts were beginning to filter through into government thinking.[15] The point was made more sharply by the then Leader of the Opposition, Neil Kinnock, in a speech in 1990: 'Anyone concerned about the future of the family', he said, 'should understand that in our generation the family is changing, it is not collapsing'.[16] Those who regarded the rise of the non-traditional family as evidence of social delinquency, he went on, showed not only prejudice but impracticality in the face of the problems accompanying change.

Behind such statements is a growing body of social research which has traced the shifts in the domestic patterns which frame sexual behaviour. In many ways, we are still deeply familial in our behaviour patterns. Although the age of marriage has crept up in recent years, most people still get married. Though there has been a recent decline, a high proportion of divorced people re-marry. And even though there is a growing percentage of children born outside marriage, they are more often than not born into marriage-like relationships. A majority of 'illegitimate births' are jointly registered by both parents. Although we are more tolerant of pre-marital sex, we remain very censorious of extra-marital sex. And the majority, as we have seen, still disapprove of homosexual relationships, and the adoption of children by lesbians and gay men. We remain, in the words of the sociologist David Clark, deeply 'Wedlocked'.[17]

Yet these overall figures conceal a great deal of variety. A survey by National Opinion Polls for the *Independent* showed that the traditional view of the family was held by only a minority, while the under-35's have a 'radically different view of family life to that of their parents' generation'. These different views of the under-35s include a more relaxed attitude to both partners working, joint rearing of children, and a more tolerant attitude (though still only amongst about a third of those polled) to homosexual adoptions.[18]

But beyond such generational shifts is a growing recognition that the word 'family' covers a multitude of forms. In the early 1980s the family sociologists Rhona and Robert Rappoport distinguished five types of family diversity: by internal organisation of the family; as a result of cultural factors such as race and ethnicity, religious and other factors; class differences in family life; changes over the life-course; and differing patterns by generation. Others have listed different types of 'families', ranging from non-married cohabitation to single parenthood, from 'commuter-marriages' to lesbian and gay relationships.[19] As we know, the latter were labelled 'pretended family relationships' in the Local Government Act of 1988, but once you broaden the definition of the family to include non-traditional forms, it is difficult to know what you can legitimately exclude.

The point I am making is that sexual activity, and committed sexual-emotional relationships, take place today in a number of more or less long term settings, and have given rise to a range of patterns of domestic organisation. We have not yet sorted out, however, the implications of this for policy or ideology. We know, for example, that many women choose single-parenthood. We also know that more often than not single-parenthood is associated with poverty. The Conservative government in 1990 announced proposals for making errant fathers contribute to the rearing of children, presumably as one sort of response to poverty. But little thought has been given to the implications of that response to the question of choice.[20] More often than not we continue to pay lip-service to individual freedom while being punitive to those who exercise it.

These are difficult issues, but ones which, I believe, will dominate the social agenda in the 1990s. They are likely to shift us away from a moral politics which relies on *a priori* positions towards one which looks at needs and how they can be satisfied. Put another way, we are likely to see less and less emphasis on moral absolutes and an increasing willingness to live with moral diversity.

The Impacts of AIDS

Finally, I want to look at an experience which has fed into the moral absolutism of the 1980s, threatened to create a sort of backlash against sexual liberalism, and has had a tragic effect on the lives of many people – the impact of the health crisis associated with HIV disease, and AIDS.

The response to HIV has been coloured by the fact that it has been seen as a disease, in the west at least, of the marginal and the execrated. In America and Britain – but not, it must be said, in all European countries – largely, it has so far affected gay men and intravenous drug users, the so called 'guilty victims' compared to supposedly 'innocent victims' such as haemophiliacs. It was only when it seemed that HIV was likely to seep through into the heterosexual community that governments in the USA and Britain displayed any urgency on the matter. The British government's launch into urgent action at the end of 1986 was precipitated by the US Surgeon-General's report on the danger of a heterosexual epidemic earlier that year. A tailing off in urgency followed in 1989 after reports circulated that rumours of a heterosexual threat were much exaggerated. It seems that urgency is not required if only unpopular minorities are at risk.[21]

But, and it should not need saying, we are complacent about the risks of HIV and AIDS at our peril. In Africa and other parts of the developing world millions are at risk. In the USA well over 100,000 people have been diagnosed with AIDS, more than half are dead. HIV disease is the largest single cause of premature death amongst men and women in cities like New York. It is estimated that one in four American families have already been personally affected. In Britain at the time of writing nearly 6,500 have been diagnosed with AIDS, some 4,000 are dead. And the most recent figures are ominous. AIDS cases amongst heterosexuals are now rising faster than amongst any other category. The figures amongst heterosexuals are still very small in Britain, about the same as they were amongst homosexual men in 1984. But that itself indicates the dangers.[22]

The problem is that the population as a whole seems pretty resistant to warnings about these dangers. The gay community quite early on learnt the need for safer-sex techniques, and the avoidance of high-risk activities. The results were seen in a drop of Sexually Transmitted Disease (STD) infections amongst gay men in the late 1980s, and a slowing down of the expected rate of increase of infection. But there is no similar evidence for a widespread adoption of safer sex amongst heterosexuals. Recent STD figures suggest, moreover, a dangerous increase again of infections. In one London hospital, gonorrhoea infections rose by almost 100 per cent between 1988 and 1990. It seems that people are becoming complacent about the dangers.[23]

This suggests that the doom-laden warnings that have characterised much of the public education on AIDS are not effective. Equally ineffective, however, were the calls for a re-moralisation of behaviour that we heard in the 1980s. There was certainly, as we have seen, a renewed hostility towards homosexuality, and this had very unpleasant effects. A recent *British Social Attitudes* survey indicated that there has been a slight decline in the tendency to see AIDS in moral terms, though there remains strong support for statements that certain sexual practices are morally wrong.[24] Yet there is overwhelming evidence that this does not stop people doing them. What such moralism does do, however, is prevent the full dissemination of knowledge about risk activities and safer-sex techniques.

That moralism is not surprising, however, because the HIV/AIDS crisis dramatizes many of the uncertainties and ambiguities that are shaping sexual mores at the end of this century. It feeds into that sense of an end of an era which I have already noted as an important component of our culture at the present. It dramatizes the existence of sexual and cultural diversity. It underlines the absence of a consensus concerning what is ethically valid and invalid, acceptable or unacceptable, right and wrong. People with HIV and AIDS have had to endure stigma because our culture has been unable to come to terms with the changes that have transformed sexual life in the twentieth century.

I have suggested in this chapter that sexual behaviour and sexual beliefs are being shaped and re-shaped by a number of long-term trends: secularisation, liberalisation, and the growth of social and moral diversity. During the 1980s, under the impact both of political forces and of AIDS, a number of these trends seemed to be on the point of going into reverse. But it is already looking as if these were blips rather than fundamental shifts. If this is so, then we need to adjust to these trends in our thinking about sexuality. It's time, I suggest, that our moral systems begin to move closer to what we actually do and are, rather than what inherited traditions say we should do and be. If that were to happen we would, I believe, see the development not only of a more humane and tolerant culture, but one that was also more responsible and healthier in facing the challenges of this particular *fin de siècle*.

Notes

[1] Further details for the examples given can be found in Jeffrey Weeks, *Sex, Politics*

and Society: The Regulation of Sexuality since 1800, 2nd edition, Longman, Harlow 1989.

[2] On homosexuality see the title essay in David M. Halperin, *One Hundred Years of Homosexuality, and Other Essays on Greek Love*, Routledge, New York and London 1990; Eve Kosovsky Sedgwick, *Epistemology of the Closet*, University of California Press, Berkeley and Los Angeles 1990; and the essays in Jeffrey Weeks, *Against Nature: Essays on History, Sexuality and Identity*, Rivers Oram Press, London 1991.

[3] On this theme, see Elaine Showalter, *Sexual Anarchy: Gender and Culture at the Fin de Siècle*, Bloomsbury, London 1991.

[4] On the 'sexual tradition', see Jeffrey Weeks, *Sexuality and its Discontents: Meanings, Myths and Modern Sexualities*, Routledge, London and New York 1985.

[5] Interview with Sir Immanual Jakobovits, *Independent*, 27 November 1987.

[6] See coverage of the 1992 convention in the newspapers of August 1992.

[7] See Weeks, *Sexuality and its Discontents*, chapter 4; and Jeffrey Weeks, *Sexuality*, Ellis Horwood/Tavistock, Chichester and London 1986, chapter 6.

[8] On this theme see Anthony Giddens, *The Transformation of Intimacy, Sexuality, Love and Eroticism in Modern Societies*, Polity Press, Cambridge 1992.

[9] On the Thatcher years see Martin Durham, *Sex and Politics: The Family and Morality in the Thatcher Years*, Macmillan, Basingstoke 1991.

[10] See, for example, Roger Jowell, Sharon Witherspoon, Lindsay Brook (eds), *British Social Attitudes – the 7th Report*, Gower, Aldershot 1990; *Regional Trends 25*, HMSO, London 1990; *Family Change and Future Policy*, Family Policy Studies Centre, London 1990; *Key Population and Vital Statistics 1989*, HMSO, London 1990; *Population Trends 61*, HMSO, London 1990; *Single Person Households – Single Living, Diverse Lifestyles 1992*, Mintel International Group, London 1992, quoted in *The Times*, 15 September 1992.

[11] Roger Jowell et al (eds), *British Social Attitudes. The 5th Report*, Gower, Aldershot 1988; Gallop Poll reported in the *Sunday Telegraph*, 5 June 1988.

[12] On the Wolfenden strategy and its implications see Jeffrey Weeks, *Coming Out: Homosexual Politics in Britain from the Nineteenth Century to the Present*, 2nd edition, Quartet Books, London 1990, chapter 15; Weeks, *Sex, Politics and Society*, chapter 12.

[13] Stephen Jeffery-Poulter, *Peers, Queers and Commons: The Struggle for Gay Law Reform from 1950 to the Present*, Routledge, London and New York 1991, chapter 11; Antony Grey, *Quest for Justice: Towards Homosexual Emancipation*, Sinclair-Stevenson, London 1992, pp233-5: Jeffrey Weeks, 'Pretended Family Relationships', chapter 8 in Jeffrey Weeks, *Against Nature: Essays on History, Sexuality and Identity*, Rivers Oram Press, London 1991.

[14] See for example, Sheila Jeffreys, *Anti-climax*, Pandora, London 1991 for an argument about the limitations of liberalization. For an alternative feminist argument see the two books by Lynne Segal, *Is the Future Female? Troubled Thoughts on Contemporary Feminism*, Virago, London 1987, and *Slow Motion, Changing Masculinities, Changing Men*, Virago, London 1990.

[15] Patrick Wintour, 'Changing attitudes shake family values', *Guardian*, 9 October 1990; Judy Jones, 'Minister urges need to target resources', *Independent*, 22 October 1990.

[16] Jack O'Sullivan, 'Labour stakes claim to be party for community care', *Independent*, 21 September 1990; news report of Kinnock's speech, *Guardian*, 21 September 1990.

[17] David Clark and Douglas Haldane, *Wedlocked?*, Polity Press, Cambridge 1990.

[18] Peter Kellner, 'Traditional view of family "held by minority of people" ', *Independent*, 21 September 1990.

[19] Robert and Rhona Rapoport, 'British Families in Transition', in R.N. Rapoport, M.P. Fogarty and R. Rapoport (eds), *Families in Britain*, Routledge and Kegan Paul, London 1982. See the discussion of this theme in Weeks, 'Pretended Family Relationships', op cit.

[20] For the effects of that policy see Sally Malcolm-Smith, 'Single mothers harassed to name absent fathers', *Observer*, 22 September 1991.

[21] 'AIDS: the intellectual agenda', chapter 7 in Weeks, *Against Nature*; Virginia Berridge and Philip Strong, 'AIDS policies in the UK: a preliminary analysis', in Elizabeth Fee and Daniel Fox, *AIDS: Contemporary History*, University of California Press, Berkeley 1991.

[22] For up to date figures see *WorldAIDS*, Panos Institute, London, continuing.

[23] For a commentary on changing figures see Graham Hart, Mary Boulton, Ray Fitzpatrick, John McLean and Jill Dawson ' "Relapse" to unsafe sexual behaviour amongst gay men: a critique of recent behavioural HIV/AIDS research', *Sociology of Health and Illness: A Journal of Medical Sociology*, volume 14, no 2, June 1992, pp216-32.

[24] Roger Jowell, Sharon Witherspoon and Linday Brook (eds), *British Social Attitudes – the 7th Report*, Gower, Aldershot 1991: see chapter by Kaye Wellings and Jane Wadsworth.

Outlaws as Legislators: Feminist Anti-Censorship Politics and Queer Activism

ANNA MARIE SMITH

PUSSY (Perverts Undermining State ScrutinY) was a feminist anti-censorship sub-group within OutRage!, the queer direct action group based in London. We were a unique combination of activists. Launched under the slogans, 'PUSSY Rules the World'[1] and 'Boy Pussy and Chicks with Dicks – Working Together', PUSSY included lesbian members of Feminists Against Censorship, lesbian writers, artists and cultural workers, women sex trade workers, and gay men from OutRage! Our group emerged in the summer of 1991 in response to the censorship of Della Grace's book of lesbian photography, *Love Bites*, and the second issue of the lesbian sex magazine, *Quim*. By the end of the summer, we had also contributed to Jenny White's defence campaign, initiated a dialogue on censorship among lesbian and gay publishers and bookshops, intervened in the debate on the Labour Party's position on pornography and censorship and highlighted the importance of struggling against sexism within the gay male culture. In this chapter I shall offer my own account of PUSSY's activities, with a special emphasis on the broader issues surrounding our brief campaign.

Our most difficult task was the effective communication of our *specific* anti-censorship position. We tried to link the struggle against state censorship with the struggle against censorship in lesbian and gay spaces and we tried to promote a feminist critique of censorship which remained critical of sexism and the libertarian laissez-faire approach. We did not always succeed, for we were often misunderstood. Some OutRage! members thought that we should have focused exclusively on exposing the practices of the Obscene Publications Squad of the Metropolitan Police, some feminists thought that we, the lesbians in the group, had given up our feminism, and some gay men thought that because they had joined us in our fight against the pro-censorship feminists, they had earned the right to dismiss feminism as a whole.

Queer Spaces: An Innocent Outside or a Pseudo-State?

It may be useful to clarify the complexities of our situation by developing some theoretical analogues. The arguments of many of our opponents can be depicted in terms of the 'domination/liberation' model. Our discourse differed in both *content* and *form*; it can be depicted in terms of the 'hegemony' model.[2] The 'domination/liberation' model is central to many modernist conceptions of political struggle. It represents the social – individuals, groups, communities, and institutions – as an all encompassing struggle between two fundamental camps. In the modernist moment in Marx's discourse, for example, he claims that the social will ultimately take the form of an all-out struggle between the bourgeoisie and the proletariat. Our opponents similarly presumed that the censorship struggle was basically a two-camp total war. Underlying the pro-censorship feminists' position was the assumption that the world was divided into a total struggle between the sexists and the anti-sexists. Because they defined explicit material as *the* exemplary sexist text, they placed us, the defenders of explicit lesbian material, on the side of the sexists. The arguments of our sexist gay male critics rested on the assumption that the world was divided into the pro-gay freedom versus the anti-gay freedom camps. Because they had not taken on board the feminist critique of their sexism, they viewed that critique as a puritan attack on sexual freedom. When we voiced our pro-sex lesbian position, they jumped to the conclusion that we were with them on the pro-gay freedom side, against the feminists. In other words, the 'domination/liberation' model cannot accommodate multiple divisions and contradictory identifications. From this perspective, one simply cannot both support lesbian sexual explicitness and fight against sexism. Because our opponents adopted this way of thinking about their politics, their discourse contributed to the erasure of our feminism.

The 'domination/liberation' model also reduces the oppressed side of the two camp divide to a wholly disempowered innocence. If the 'dominant' camp is the 'inside' – the empowered, the represented, the owners of the political terrain – then the 'oppressed' camp is the 'outside' – the disempowered, the unrepresented, the dispossessed. In this model, the Law is supposed to operate purely in terms of the interests of the 'inside'. The 'outsiders' are 'outlaws': they are excluded by law from the 'inside' space, and, because they do not own the means of discursive production, because they cannot be represented in the 'inside''s courts of law, they do not participate in any way in the production of laws. They are nothing but the ruled, and do not themselves become rulers, not even in their own 'outside' space, for their 'outside' space is a non-space. 'Outsiders', then, such as the anti-sexists in the pro-censorship feminist model, or the pro-gay freedom side in the sexist gay male model, are innocent: robbed of virtually all political power, they remain essentially the oppressed, and in no way reproduce the legislating activity of their oppressors.

The 'outsiders', however, are not doomed to perpetual oppression in the 'domination/liberation' model. Because the 'insider' culture remains a separate space from the 'outside', 'outsiders' retain their true identity. Domination by the 'inside' may distort or conceal that true self, but ultimately, the 'outsider''s truth can be recovered in its pure form. In these terms, then, it becomes perfectly legitimate to speak of the 'true interests' of women around pornography, for example, and to dismiss all opposing views as the product of sexist thinking. The task of the 'outsider' activists is merely to lead the other 'outsiders' to take up what the activists have already identified as their true position. The 'domination/liberation' model, then, licenses an extremely arrogant and anti-democratic form of political organizing, that of the vanguard group which speaks for the rest of the oppressed and dismisses dissenting views as untruths. As I shall argue below, we encountered a particularly striking form of this arrogance when we criticized the pro-censorship position of the Campaign for Press and Broadcasting Freedom.

The 'hegemony' model depicts the social in a radically different manner. Instead of the all-encompassing 'us' versus 'them' or 'inside/outside' divisions of the 'domination/liberation' model, the 'hegemony' model represents the social as a complex field which is organized in terms of multiple and constantly shifting micro-centres of power. The de-centred operation of power ensures the permanent vulnerability of even the most empowered, and the potential for subversion on the part of the disempowered. The complex, rather than one-dimensional, character of social oppositions renders the formation of a 'natural' alliance impossible: an ally in one context may become an opponent in the next context. Above all, the 'hegemony' model rejects the political assessment system which is inherent in the 'domination/liberation' model. We cannot predict the ways in which multiple identities will be combined together in taking a position on one particular subject. For example, just because the Labour Party tends towards leftist positions, such as the defence of the national health system or the defence of the trade unions, does not mean that it will naturally take a progressive position on lesbian and gay issues. Apparently contradictory combinations, such as a racist queer activism, an anti-queer feminism or an anti-censorship *and* anti-sexist lesbian activism, are not ruled out of order by the 'hegemony' model. Instead of erasing the complexities of multiple identifications as unthinkable, the 'hegemony' model brings them to the forefront of political analysis.

The rejection of the simple two-camp model also entails the rejection of the idea that the oppressed remain isolated from the rest of the social. The reproduction of the discourse of the oppressors by the oppressed is not only a distinct possibility – in fact, mimicry and parody may be the only way in which the oppressed can organize their resistance. If the very category, homosexuality, was invented in the nineteenth century by discourses which often had oppressive effects, it nevertheless did provide the emerging sexual minorities with a way of speaking which allowed them to defend their rights. The term 'queer' has also been borrowed from anti-homosexual discourse and transformed into a statement of defiance. The reappropriation of 'queer', like that of 'homosexual', subverts bigotry by turning bigoted language against itself. 'Queer', and OutRage! slogans such as 'Queer As Fuck!', announce to both the straight bigots and the homosexual men and women who are content to work toward their inclusion in an otherwise unchanged sexist, racist, class oppressive society that queer activists are taking a militant anti-assimilationist stance.

Some queer activists may position themselves as a radically new generation, but we are actually reiterating appropriation tactics which are as old as homosexuality itself, and reoccupying positions which have already been prepared by black power activists, sexual liberationists and radical feminists. In the late 1960s, when the Labour government caved in to the anti-black immigration lobby and passed explicitly racist immigration laws, and Enoch Powell demonstrated the extent to which extremist racism had become legitimatized in post-colonial Britain, black activists responded by forming militant black power groups. White liberals had virtually dominated the 'coloured people's' organizations; the Racial Adjustment Society (RAAS) refused to allow them to join. Community organizations which participated in the Labour government's programmes were barred from the Black People's Alliance. Black militants jettisoned the terms, 'coloured' and 'Negro', just as contemporary queers have rejected the 'homosexual' and 'lesbian and gay' terms. Sivanandan comments,

> The liberal, fearful of the backlash people, points out the 'Black Power' itself is an offensive, sympathy-losing phrase. 'Coloured Power' perhaps, or 'Negro Power' would have been so much more palatable to the white power structure and less disturbing to the white psyche. But this again is the white man's problem – for, the connotations of 'Black', created by the white man himself are so frightening, so evil, so primordial that to associate it with power as well is to invoke the nightmare world of divine retribution, of Judgment Day.[3]

The self-articulation of 'queer' with pride, strength and activism similarly harnesses the forces of disgust and terror and re-directs that tremendous energy right back against its bigoted source. This re-naming is not an act of self-loathing but a collective working through of our own internalized oppression. Above all, to say, 'We're here, we're queer, get used to it', is to assert that anti-queer bigotry and institutionalized heterosexism remain the straight person's problem.

Explicit lesbian sexual representations also depend on appropriation in that they borrow extensively from mainstream sexist pornography. To the extent that the conventions of the *Playboy* pin-up are mocked in the pages of lesbian publications such as *Quim* or *On Our Backs*, this borrowing becomes subversive. Borrowing is in fact crucial to resistance discourse: if we abandoned sexual explicitness to sexist pornography we would be closing off a vital area of political struggle from feminist intervention. Borrowing also weakens the frontier between the 'inside' and the 'outside', and it is this frontier which is supposed to guarantee the innocence of the oppressed. Resistance involves constant rule-making processes whose specificities will always escape universal formulae: we are always trying to distinguish between legitimate and illegitimate borrowings from hegemonic discourse. To resist hegemonic discourse, we build spaces and institutions, and we invent rituals and codes. However, our queer spaces are precisely the same as all other socio-political spaces in that they depend on exclusions and normalizations. Our queer spaces only become bounded spaces because we, the excluded, exclude something else in turn; our positions only become intelligible because we, the transgressors, relegate something else to the sphere of the unthinkable.

If censorship is a practice which rules marginal discourse out of order by excluding it from the sphere of legitimate discourse, then censorship is not practised by the state alone. Lesbian and gay spaces reproduce state censorship in the very moment of their creation. In other words, we simply cannot escape the fact that although we may appear to be 'outlaws', we are all legislators. In the case of sexually explicit lesbian texts, the threat of censorship in Britain emerges from outside *and* within our own pseudo-state.[4] Pro-censorship lesbian feminists have dismissed those of us who defend these texts as male-defined promoters of sexism and violence against women. They continue to attempt to ban our representations from bookshops, and to exclude us from demonstrations, community centres, clubs, employments in women's organizations and housing in women's housing associations. As long as this kind of lesbian self-policing operates, groups such as PUSSY cannot pretend that lesbians and gays are all equally disempowered and that we are all innocent inhabitants of a non-space; a queer campaign against censorship has to recognize that some lesbians and gays have everything invested in the reproduction of state-like institutions within our own communities.

With the multiple fracturing of our identifications, the contextual specificities of our decision-making processes and the ambiguous effects of our borrowings from hegemonic discourses, the development of fundamental differences among feminists and among lesbian and gay activists is inevitable. Instead of one privileged voice which is supposed to express our true interests for us, we are confronted with a plurality of leaderships. No single group can claim to speak in our name as our natural representative or to express the one true line. We are always caught up in the Wittgensteinian bind – we cannot predict with precise accuracy how a given rule will operate in a different context, for it is always deformed with every new application. All we can do is to work with general approximations, and be constantly aware of the paradoxes around identity: the effects of identity claims will always escape our intentional control, and even the most subversive identity claim in one context may, in another context, become a rigidified barrier which excludes democratic contestation.

PUSSY Versus the State

PUSSY divided her time between official and community censorship. In defiance of customs regulations, we brought explicit gay male safer sex materials into Britain from our contacts in Canada, Germany and Australia. In our press release, we called for more government funding for explicit safer sex campaigns aimed at lesbians and gay men, and an end to the customs regulations which banned these materials from importation. The Terrence Higgins Trust, Britain's leading AIDS organization, had been criticized for its promotion of 'teenage promiscuity' and 'obscene' sexual material by a prominent conservative pressure group, Family and Youth Concern. We gave away our collection to punters at the OutRage! stall during Lesbian and Gay Pride day; we passed out hundreds of posters, comics, leaflets and pop-out cards in a few minutes. We also worked against official censorship by supporting Jenny White. Customs officers seized six lesbian sex videos which White had ordered from Good Vibrations, a feminist erotica shop in San Francisco. Although White lost her court challenge against the seizure, she won a 'moral victory': the magistrate ruled that she did not have to pay the court costs of Customs and Excise. At our picket outside the courtroom, we had to deal with police harassment; this was only the first of many similar incidents. True to the OutRage! style, many of us wore our 'Queer As Fuck' t-shirts, and several of our placards read, 'Lesbians Fuck – Get Used To It!' The police argued that an anonymous person – which they never had to produce – had taken offence at our public display of the word, 'fuck', and that we were therefore contravening Section 5 of the Public Order Act. In the end, this harassment only ensured greater t-shirt sales for OutRage! and a raised profile for PUSSY.

Our main target, in terms of official censorship, was the Labour Party. In the summer of 1991, the Conservatives consistently lagged behind Labour in the polls; many of us expected a Labour victory at the next election. It was with some concern, then, that we noted the development of a pornography censorship initiative in the Labour Party in the form of Dawn Primarolo's Location of Pornographic Materials Bill. This Bill would have restricted the sale of pornographic materials to premises which were licensed for that purpose and were barred from selling any other goods or services. It defined 'pornography' as material which 'for the purposes of sexual arousal or titillation, depicts women, or parts of women's bodies, as objects, things or commodities, or in sexually humiliating or degrading poses or being subjected to violence'. During the initial discussions around the Bill, Primarolo agreed to accept the following amendment, 'The reference to women above includes men.' Legitimated as an 'equal opportunities' amendment, this qualification ensured the inclusion of gay male material within the already broad and vague pornographic category. The Bill did not allow for any exemptions on the grounds of artistic or literary merit, public interest or HIV prevention. As a private member's Bill, it did not become law, but it did signal the possibility of future legislation under a Labour government. It was supported by Labour's strongest advocates for lesbian and gay rights, Jeremy Corbyn, Audrey Wise, Clare Short and Primarolo herself.

Primarolo defended her Bill in *Capital Gay*[5] in terms of her feminist intentions; she stressed that her Bill would not ban pornography, that pornography 'systematically degrades women', and that the critics of her Bill were 'mislead[ing] people about our intentions'. Our concern was not about Primarolo's intentions, but about the absolute irrelevance of feminist intentions in the application of such legislation, and the ways in which the Bill would be used to attack the lesbian and gay communities. It would have made the sale and distribution of many lesbian and gay publications in our bookshops, clubs and community centres illegal, and would have had disastrous effects on safer sex campaigns and sexually explicit art echibitions. If the inclusion of the amendment to her Bill is not already sufficient evidence of the fact that feminist initiatives can be thoroughly appropriated by anti-queer interests, we need only look at the situation in Canada. In February, 1992, the Canadian Supreme Court re-defined obscene material as sexual representations which 'cause harm' through 'degrading' and 'dehumanizing' portrayals, including bondage and s/m. Kathleen Mahoney, the lawyer who represented the Women's Legal Education and Action Fund in court, explained the strategy behind their 'victory'.

> We showed them the porn – and among the seized videos were some horrifically violent and degrading gay movies. We made the point that the abused men in these films were being treated like women – and the judges got it. Otherwise, men can't put themselves in our shoes. Porn makes women's subordination look sexy and appealing; it doesn't threaten men's jobs, safety, rights or credibility.[6]

In other words, LEAF did not ask the court to make the crucial distinction between sexism and sexual explicitness, two distinct elements which may or may not coincide with one another. It gave free rein to the classic anti-gay male interpretation: men being dominated and penetrated by other men are 'abused' and 'degraded' because they are being 'treated like women'. Their initiative had its origin in feminist intentions, succeeded because of the anti-gay male bigotry of the courts, and had the effect of censoring lesbian sexuality. A lesbian sex magazine, which was on sale at a lesbian and gay bookshop, was the object of the first obscenity prosecution following this decision. Glad Day bookshop in Toronto was charged for selling the American lesbian sex magazine, *Bad Attitude*, because it contained images of lesbian s/m sex.

Our PUSSY intervention in the British debate took the form of an exchange of letters in *Capital Gay*. Feminists Against Censorship were already at work lobbying Labour Party MPs but we wanted to express a specifically queer position in a queer space. Primarolo had received explicit support from Paud Hegarty, a staff member of Gay's the Word bookshop in London, and she consistently attempted to represent his view as the only lesbian and gay position. Peter Tatchell, writing as an independent gay activist, entered the debate with an opinion piece in *Capital Gay*.[7] He drew attention to the censorious effects of a future Labour government's policies on lesbian and gay venues and publications. Teresa Stratford, of the Women's Section of the Campaign for Press and Broadcasting Freedom, which – despite its name – had been involved in drafting Primarolo's Bill, responded with a letter to the editor. It was clear from this exchange that the CPBF and Labour Party MPs were concerned about lesbian and gay opinion on the matter, but that they had already dismissed the anti-censorship position as anti-feminist. Stratford charged that Tatchell's article was misogynistic because he had failed to recognize the 'fact' about pornography, namely that '83% of women feel oppressed and disadvantaged by the exploitation of our supposed sexuality in pornographic magazines'. She added that her group 'would like to work with members of the gay and lesbian community [on amending the Bill]', but that until the anti-censorship critics 'acknowledged that there is a problem for us, that we do experience an oppression here, and that help is not going to come to us from the political right, then the prospects of working out a compromise are slim'.[8]

Tatchell responded with another letter in which he deplored Stratford's use of a personal attack against him. Roz Kaveney also wrote a letter in which she rejected Stratford's association of opposition against Primarolo's Bill with misogyny, and stated that many lesbians were equally suspicious of the Bill.[9] In our PUSSY letter, we defended Tatchell's right as a gay man to voice his opinion. We argued that 'men should support feminism', but that because there are many different feminisms, 'men should inform themselves about [the censorship] debate, and take a position'.[10] We felt strongly about this aspect of the debate. It simply would not be acceptable for whites to say that they could not chose between the positions of conservative blacks and radical blacks, such as Inkatha and the ANC, or Clarence Thomas and Jesse Jackson, because they were white; to do so would be to ignore, in a racist manner, one's responsibility on a political question of crucial importance. We lesbians have taken difficult positions in debates around gay male sexuality, such as public sex and male prostitution, and we have never argued that we could not do so because they were 'male issues'. The gay men who did not take a stand were only giving their tacit approval to the pro-censorship feminists' claim that their feminism was indeed the only possible feminism.

We also took aim against Stratford's arrogant language and her use of 'majoritarian' statistics and logic. After questioning her '83%' figure, we stated,

> We resent the way that Stratford claims to be speaking for all women – many women, including lesbians, make the distinction between sexism and sexual explicitness and defend non-sexist explicit material from a feminist perspective. However, even if a majority of women did agree with Stratford's position, we would still be right to oppose this Bill. In 1988, 85.9% of the British population thought that the promotion of homosexuality should be prohibited, and many Labour MPs supported Section 28. They were wrong then, and Dawn Primarolo, Clare Short et al. are wrong now. Democracy means protecting the rights of minorities, Stratford. Don't lecture us on the meaning of the democratic tradition. The Labour Party should scrap the Primarolo Bill and stop engaging in cheap, opportunistic politics at our expense.

Stratford and Primarolo's discourse had situated Tatchell on one extreme, and the right on the other, such that the pro-censorship feminists appeared to occupy the legitimate centre. They wanted to erase the anti-censorship position as unthinkable, such that they could appear as the natural representatives of the lesbian and gay communities' true interests. By re-iterating the anti-censorship position in even stronger language, the effect of our intervention was to situate ourselves on the 'extreme', such that Tatchell's position appeared more centrist, and Stratford and Primarolo's appeared much closer to that of the sexist and anti-queer right. At the same time, we wanted to show that our 'extreme' queer position on this issue was the only legitimate position. The point here was to insist on our right to organize politically in an independent manner, to undermine the left's tendency to take lesbian and gay support for granted and to counter the left's erasure of queer militancy.

It is important to note that the Labour Party often engages in the marginalization of 'extremist' positions among women's, black and lesbian and gay leaderships. It has to do so to preserve the image of itself as the natural leaders of the 'progressive' camp in its two-camp model of the social. Roy Hattersley's response to OutRage!'s criticism of Labour's position on the reform of gay male age of consent laws in November, 1991 is but one example. OutRage! wrote to Hattersley, Labour's deputy leader, and stated that it was 'totally unacceptable and insulting to the lesbian and gay community' that a Labour government would allow a free vote, instead of applying the usual mechanisms of party discipline, for age of consent legislation. In his reply, Hattersley stated that the Labour Party would only discuss its policies with the lesbian and gay lobbying organization, Stonewall, because his Party believes it to be 'the most representative and most influential amongst gay men and lesbians'. Hattersley's spokesman stated further, OutRage! is one of the groups we feel that we don't wish to deal with at the moment, until it is able to engage in fair and rational debate.'[11] We have to be far more attentive to sophisticated strategies such as these which are used by both the right and the left to invent or to exacerbate differences within minority communities.

We also used our PUSSY letter to launch our group to the lesbian and gay public. We stated sarcastically that because the CPBF and the Labour Party would only contribute to the censorship of lesbian and gay materials, they should send their donations to our group, care of the London Lesbian and Gay Centre. *Capital Gay* gave us their full support: they positioned our letter at the top of the page and used a provocative headline, 'They're Making More Work for PUSSY'. Throughout the summer, PUSSY received total co-operation from *Capital Gay*. Unlike the *Pink Paper* and *Gay Times*, *Capital Gay* consistently covered our actions and printed several opinion pieces around censorship.

PUSSY Versus the Pseudo-State Within

PUSSY focused her attention, in terms of community censorship, on the defence of Della Grace's lesbian photography book *Love Bites*[12] and the second issue of the lesbian sex magazine *Quim*. *Love Bites* is a collection of photographs which range from straightforward documentaries of lesbian bars and demonstrations, to stylish colour portraits, to black and white images of lesbian sex. One of the latter images depicts a threesome; the models' poses – a woman draped over a leather jacket-covered stool, her mouth gasping in pleasure; another woman kneeling at her head, holding her hair and chin in a masterful grasp; and a third woman standing behind the exposed ass of the first, her hips firmly thrust forward, a glimpse of a leather harness around her, and a suggestion of a concealed dildo – gave the impression of vaginal penetration. Although there has been very little in the way of legal precedents around dildo penetration, some bookshops, such as the women's bookshop in London, Silver Moon, believed that the image could have been interpreted as obscene. Silver Moon spokespersons also stated that although they fully supported Grace's work, they could not afford to be prosecuted even if they did eventually win such a case. Other bookshops, such as Sisterwrite, refused to sell *Love Bites* because they were 'disturbed by the violent sado-masochistic imagery in this book and [did] not want to place it on shelves where other women [would be] offended by it'.[13] Gay's the Word, Britain's only lesbian and gay bookshop, remained inconsistent throughout the summer. When they did respond to our enquiries, they constantly shifted their reasons for not selling *Love Bites* back and forth between Silver Moon and Sisterwrite's positions. Some alternative bookshops, such as Compendium, stocked the book but did not want to sell it to male customers.

At the same time, *Love Bites* was freely available in high street bookshops such as Dillons and Waterstones. Grace had taken her book concept to many feminist and lesbian and gay publishers, but only Gay Men's Press had offered her a contract. Gay Men's Press publicists admitted that because of the censorship of the book in lesbian and gay bookshops, and because of the popularity of lesbian images for heterosexual male consumers, as much as 80% of the sales of *Love Bites* would be to straight men. The only lesbian and gay outlet for the book was West and Wilde in Edinburgh, which operates under Scottish obscenity legislation. When *Quim* was released in late June, it was also censored by most of the community bookshops. Silver Moon agreed to sell it because its most explicit materials were written, rather than visual, and because the Obscene Publications Squad targets photography and videos, rather than fiction. West and Wilde was once again the only lesbian and gay bookshop in the United Kingdom which stocked *Quim* without reservation.

The decisions of these bookshops were extremely important. Unlike gay male material, explicit lesbian texts and images are quite scarce, especially in Britain. We felt that because of this community censorship, *Love Bites* would be, for the most part, appropriated by straight male consumers. Although gay male imagery is of course borrowed by the straight media all the time, the threat of appropriation is particularly acute for lesbians. The most intense attacks on lesbians have been in the form of erasing lesbian sexuality as a mere pretence – as in Section 28 and the Jennifer Saunders case[14] – or as an easily assimilated titillation for male heterosexual pleasure. The specific character of anti-lesbian discourse lies in its misogynist origins: it emerges out of the sexist assumption that because women are naturally passive and dependent upon men for their very self-definition, an autonomous women's sexuality remains impossible. *Love Bites* and *Quim* are all the more valuable precisely because they work against the sexist erasure of women's autonomy and lesbian sexuality. The censorship of *Quim* also had an economic effect on its lesbian editors. As a low budget magazine, *Quim* did not receive the same mainstream attention as *Love Bites*, and it was much more dependent on community spaces for distribution. The community censorship meant that the print run for the magazine was very small, which in turn raised the cover cost. Because lesbians' income reflects the inequalities of the distribution of income in general – (women's average income still stands at about 60% of men's average income) – the economic factors in lesbian publishing are crucial to the success of small ventures such as *Quim*.

PUSSY's first priority on this issue was to sell as many copies of *Love Bites* and *Quim* to lesbians as possible. By appearing in the lesbian and gay press virtually on a weekly basis throughout the summer, we kept these texts in the headlines. We sold both the book and the magazine at the OutRage! stalls at Lesbian and Gay Pride. At every possible opportunity, we told lesbians the names of the bookshops which were selling *Love Bites* and *Quim*. By mid-summer *Love Bites* had risen to the top of the alternative bookshops' sales list in *City Limits* and Silver Moon had placed a second order for extra copies of *Quim*.

We also wanted to question the bookshops' policies and to open a broader dialogue on censorship. Working closely with Della Grace, Gay Men's Press and the editors of *Quim*, we contacted the bookshops and asked them to clarify their policies. Some of our critics thought that we were going to call for a boycott, but this strategy was never actually considered. At the height of a recession, and after more than ten years of the Thatcherite attack on our lesbian and gay communities, we hardly wanted to contribute to the closure of these vitally important spaces. But we did want the bookshops to recognize the diversity of the lesbian and gay communities and the importance of these lesbian texts. PUSSY asked every member of OutRage! – the main group's meeting had about sixty gay men and ten lesbians in attendance every week – to telephone Silver Moon, Gay's the Word and Sisterwrite and to ask them to stock both texts. We organized a bookshop tour which we called 'PUSSY On the Prowl'. Using the slogan, 'Fight Sexism, Promote Sex', we attempted to give our action a specifically pro-sex feminist orientation. Because we did not want to be mistaken as a picket outside the bookshops, we adopted a queer street theatre approach. We carried balloons as well as placards, we brought dogs and portable tape decks with dance music, several of the lesbians wore leather and lace club gear, and one gay man did the whole tour in a full-length wedding gown and high heels. When we arrived at each bookshop, we encouraged passers-by to patronize the shop, and we questioned punters on the way out about their views on censorship.

After the bookshop tour, we organized an open forum on censorship. It was attended by representatives of Silver Moon and Sisterwrite, Compendium and Central Books, Gay Men's Press, Sheba Feminist Publishers, *Square Peg* – a lesbian and gay alternative art magazine, *Rouge* – a lesbian and gay monthly magazine, Feminists Against Censorship, Della Grace, the *Quim* editors and OutRage! members. Letters and messages from Frontline Books in Manchester and West and Wilde were also read to the meeting. Lesbian writer Cherry Smyth gave the forum high marks in her report in *Capital Gay*: 'One of the successes of the meeting was the atmosphere of respect and mutual listening among opposing factions, who accepted ideological differences without acrimony or dismissal ... The mixed gender and politics of the meeting suggest a huge leap forward in lesbian and gay strategies towards a diversity of radical, progressive alliance.'[15] Feminists Against Censorship also organized a similar open forum in the autumn of 1991.

'Same Old Shit, Different Boys': PUSSY Bites Back

Smyth is right to emphasize the mixed gender of our PUSSY actions; in London, cross-gender solidarity in lesbian and gay politics is extremely rare. I think that it would be fair to say that many gay male activists experienced PUSSY as a liberating experience. They often told me that they had thought that feminists basically wanted them to keep quiet and get out of the way. When we asked them to look at lesbian images, buy our lesbian texts, demand that they be stocked in our bookshops and support us on our actions, many of them responded with a really positive political commitment. Journalists such as Paul Burston also addressed the gender cross-over which characterized the very texts which we were promoting. In a review of *Love Bites*, Burston courageously explored the possibility that Grace's photographs could be taken up as erotic icons for gay men as well as lesbians. He offered several tentative suggestions:

> Could it be that gender-bending traditions of both our communities, coupled with the disruption of gender-norms through parody (the masquerade of exaggerated masculinity, the fetish of extreme femininity) have led to the creation of a realm of erotic fantasy wherein sexual and gender boundaries can be crossed? Could we be talking about the possibility of a shared homo-erotic space?[16]

35

Pleasure Principles

Burston's prediction has actually come true. *Sadie Maisie's*, the first s/m and fetish club for both lesbians and gay men in Britain, opened at the London Lesbian and Gay Centre in the autumn of 1991. Many of the male punters seem to share Burston's interest in promoting lesbian and gay male erotic borrowing. When asked why they preferred this modest venue to some of the larger men-only spaces, they told me that the men at *Sadie Maisie's* tended to be far more warm and open, and far less interested in rigid hyper-masculine posing. All of them attributed this difference in atmosphere to the significant presence of lesbians, and the absence of the anti-lesbian, gay-men-plus-straight-women groups which dominate London's other mixed clubs.

For many of us lesbians, PUSSY was a rare opportunity to work and to socialize with some quite simply fabulous gay men. There were, however, serious limitations to gay men's support, both inside and outside OutRage!. A small group of gay men in OutRage! thoroughly resented the way in which we lesbians did not just keep ourselves to ourselves in a woman-only caucus, but organized a high profile anti-censorship sub-group that was, by design, lesbian dominated. Although I do not object to women-only organizing in the least, this male separatist promotion of women-only groups should be noted. Some of these male separatists did support PUSSY, but for all the wrong reasons; for them, our criticism of a particular type of feminism amounted to an attack on feminism as a whole. They championed our struggle in the same way that the right champions misogynist lesbians like Camille Paglia or anti-affirmative action blacks like Clarence Thomas: they thought that we could be used as local allies in the fight against feminism. As the *Quim* women put it, in their inimitable style,

Same old shit, different boys
There's a different brand of boy around at the moment who reckon that just because you're a pro-sex dyke, maybe don a bit of leather, and talk brash and bold on occasion, that you have forgotten your feminism and they can get away with sexist put downs, anti-women jokes and all the rest of it. It's as if they think there are two kinds of dykes, the 'old kind' who got on their nerves with their 'excuse me, that's the third time you've interrupted me' and some new kind which they reckon is me. I've been in rooms, too often recently, with gay men who assumed, until set

36

straight, that they could get snide about the 'feminist kind of lesbian' and I'd laugh along. These boys should remember that despite our differences, and the variations in our backgrounds/perspectives, we all have something in common and it begins with a 'W' and doesn't have a dick. (Unless it lives in a toy box and straps on, of course.)[17]

Over the summer, many of us became increasingly frustrated with these sexist gay male separatists, and our image of cross-gender solidarity lost much of its original appeal. I began the summer absolutely opposed to the organization of women-only groups in OutRage!, and to the scheduling of meetings in the women-only bar in our community centre. By August, I had become an enthusiastic supporter of the new lesbian caucus, LABIA (Lesbians Answer Back In Anger), as well as working-class and black caucuses. I have also become convinced that groups which are 'mixed', in terms of races, genders, sexualities, and so on, should not focus on numbers. All too often, a well-intentioned gay man would note the relative scarcity of women at the main OutRage! meetings (most of the women in PUSSY either felt that they were too busy to attend the main meetings, or that the main meetings were irrelevant to their interests), and other gay men would respond with suggestions for better advertising for the meetings. This approach could hardly be more inappropriate: radical diversity is not just a matter of public relations; it requires a lot of hard work. We white queers have to deal with our racism, and we have to transform our entire political agenda if we want black queers to commit themselves to the very difficult labour of working in white-dominated organizations. Similarly, the presence of lesbians in mixed gender groups has to be earned through substantial efforts on the part of gay men to confront their own investment in sexist privileges and institutions. A focus on numbers alone puts far too much pressure on the few women and the few blacks who do make the attempt to work in 'mixed' groups, and diverts attention from the more intractable problem of the institutionalization of oppression within our own queer spaces.

Our last PUSSY action had, in fact, very little to do with censorship. The Brief Encounter, a bar in Soho which caters mostly to the West End gay male crowd, casually announced that it was going to organize regular 'Bring a Fish' nights – meaning that on those nights, gay men were encouraged to bring a woman friend. We seized this opportunity to remind our supporters that our campaign against censorship was first and foremost a feminist campaign. PUSSY organized a zap of the bar: we disrupted it on a busy night for about a half an hour by blowing whistles, waving cardboard fish and distributing leaflets with the slogan 'The Fish Are Biting!'. As we expected, the management remained absolutely unimpressed with our intervention, but our action became a valuable photo opportunity which allowed us to publicize our feminist critique of gay male culture.

At the end of the summer, I wrote a short statement for a photographic exhibition by Della Grace at the Metro Cinema in London called 'Beauty's Eye'. In writing this piece, I was acutely aware of the fact that through Grace's work, lesbian sexuality had indeed achieved some degree of visibility – several reviews in popular magazines, an afternoon session at the Institute of Contemporary Arts, a panel at 'Body Politic: Erotic Self ', a *Marxism Today* forum and a launch at the Photographers' Gallery has been devoted to Grace's book, and now a new selection of her lesbian portraits was on view for a largely heterosexual audience in a West End cinema. This statement is perhaps the best record of my own ambivalence about the new lesbian visibility and the PUSSY experience in general.

Beauty's Eye
The 'traditional' eye of beauty is open, inviting and sexually available to the viewer. But at the same time, just as the viewer is invited into that anxiety-laced terrain of the sexual, the 'traditional' eye of beauty is also fundamentally reassuring. Whether it is the look of the page three pin-up 'girl', the soft focus of David Hamilton-type femininity, or the images in mainstream fashion magazines, the viewer is assured that there will be nothing new here, nothing unsettling, nothing which threatens to break the rules. The 'traditional' eye promises that the feminine aperture has already been colonized – come on in, we won't bite back – and the image keeps the promise.

The eye of beauty in Della Grace's photographs is also open and also issues a sexual invitation. The lighting techniques, the textures and the lines of the composition all collude to draw the viewer in.

Even in the 'Ruff Sex' sequence, in which the models appear to be spontaneously acting out their own scripts, Grace's camera does not merely record, but frames images with striking attention to textures and forms.

Grace's invitation is legible and seductive for the viewer because, in a certain way, all this has been seen before – isn't that the knife blade of Mapplethorpe, aren't the poses, the tattoos and the leather gear borrowed from women sex trade workers and gay male pornography, haven't some of those styles already appeared in post-punk fashion?

The traditional reassurance, however, is missing. In its place, the models in Grace's photographs state their defiance – 'we know you're watching, we have in fact set you up to watch us, we're getting off on your voyeurism, but if you want to play with us, the play will be organized on our terms, according to our rules'. Does it need to be said that these women *remain* lesbians, even as they exhibit their sexuality to you? The risk is displaced onto the viewer – you are invited to look, and to become seduced by this subversive type of beauty, but you are also confronted with the possibility that we have been using your gaze for our own amusement, and that as we move on to our next sex game, we have already left you behind.

Notes

[1] This line was taken from the Arena television documentary on Madonna. When she was asked why a black cat was featured in her 'Express Yourself' video, she replied, 'Pussy rules the world.'

[2] In constructing these two theoretical models, I have drawn extensively on the theories of Michel Foucault (*The History of Sexuality*, New York, Random House, 1980), Ernesto Laclau and Chantal Mouffe (*Hegemony and Socialist Strategy*, London, Verso, 1985), and Judith Butler (*Gender Trouble*, London, Routledge, 1990).

[3] A Sivanandan, *A Different Hunger: Writings on Black Resistance*, London, Pluto Press, 1982, p 66.

[4] This is not to say, however, that lesbian publications are not subject to actual criminal legislation and customs regulations. *On Our Backs* and lesbian sex videos are virtually banned from importation into Britain, and several bookshops anticipate increased attention to explicit lesbian materials on the part of the Obscene Publications Squad of the Metropolitan Police.

[5] 3 May 1991, 1.

[6] Quoted in *Ms*, May/June 1992, p 14.

[7] 17 May 1991, p 18.

[8] *Capital Gay*, 31 May 1991, p 2.

[9] *Capital Gay*, 7 June 1991, p 2.

[10] *Capital Gay*, 14 June 1991, p 2.

[11] *Capital Gay*, 15 November 1991, pp 1,4.

[12] Della Grace, *Love Bites* Éditions Aubrey Walters, London, 1991.

[13] Press release, Sisterwrite, 18 June 1991.

[14] Under Section 28, the 'promotion of homosexuality as a pretended family relationship' by local governments is illegal. Several MPs referred to lesbian parents as 'pretenders' during the parliamentary debates of this measure. Section 28 therefore legitimates one of the most serious attacks by the state against lesbians, namely the violation of lesbians' rights to child custody and to access to artificial insemination. Jennifer Saunders was sentenced to six years in prison for 'assaultintg' her female sex partners. Saunders used a male disguise to conceal the lesbian character of her relationships from her partners' families. Against her protests to the contrary, the prosecution successfully argued that her partners had never known that she was a woman, and that they had therefore not given her their informed consent. She was immediately released several months later after a successful appeal.

[15] *Capital Gay*, 19 July 1991, p 11.

[16] *Capital Gay*, 21 June 1991, p 17.

[17] *Quim*, no. 3, winter, 1991, p 5.

Women's Art Practice/ Man's Sex ... and now for something completely different[1]

NAOMI SALAMAN

I have been researching an exhibition of photographic work by women looking at men. The idea for the exhibition comes after a decade of strident feminist and right-wing anti-pornography campaigns. The aim of the exhibition, called *What She Wants* (WSW), is to present an experimental reversal of erotic traditions from women artists, to give a platform to women artists and photographers whose work is, in theme or visual content, about the erotics of looking at men.[2] This includes the process of actually taking the pictures as well as exploring the fears and taboos of showing explicit images of the male body.

While there has been a considerable amount of interesting work done in feminist theory and art practice concerning the construction of femininity, the representation of women and the 'male' gaze, there has been much less work which focuses on female spectatorship and representations of masculinity. As feminist art critiques developed from the question 'why have there been no great women artists?'[3] so the WSW project begins with the question 'why have there been no great women visual pornographers?'

The supplementary question 'what is pornography for women?' is not new, but until recently it has not been given much serious attention. The anti-pornography feminist concern has been about regulating men's access to certain types of images of women, whilst anti-censorship groups have often concentrated on defending and celebrating gay sexualities and on countering police and state homophobia. Whilst gay and lesbian voices have been forthright in defending their sexuality as a right, straight feminism has been divided and confused. In this article I want to point to some of the more persistent arguments in the anti-pornography campaigns, to relate them to a blind spot in the theory and practice of women looking at men and to hint at some of the difficulties of representing the man's sex.

The WSW exhibition is of most interest to women who have sexual pleasure with men but whatever your sexual persuasion, or gender, you may enjoy fantasies about the male body.[4] As part of my work for the exhibition I produced a research questionnaire about images of men. The cover has a picture of a dildo and underneath it says 'ceci n'est pas un penis.' I wanted to use a photograph of a dildo to talk about erections, desire, the phallus and the image. The Magritte reference is a way of implicating the mesh of fantasy in looking and language. In Magritte's famous painting of the pipe, 'The Treason of Images', neither the image nor the text contain the pipe but both circulate a fantasy about it. In the dildo card I play on this not-being-it, in terms of the absent object. While we can argue that the dildo is not the penis is not the phallus, fantasies about the body connect these terms as does the way they can temporarily stand in for one another.

The history of how the dildo card got made gives a twist to the idea of the absent object. Della Grace, the photographer, agreed to photograph her Jeff Striker dildo for me. She sent the prints in the post. They never arrived. She sent some more. They also failed to materialise. I noticed that all my post was arriving pre-opened. I had rung the Vice Squad and the Home Office a few weeks earlier to ask them about interpretations of the obscenity legislation. They took my telephone number and thus had access to my address.

So I met Della in town and she passed me the prints. I felt as though we were going to get busted, all for a photo of a dildo! Next I went to a bureau to scan the image onto disk. When I returned to have it output on bromide the computer refused to read the dildo image and kept printing out a black page with blank space. One of the workers was able to find the original scanned image but I had lost the manipulation, scaling and shading work I had done to it, so he redid it for me. He sat at the screen smiling, professing his love and knowledge of the male anatomy while he performed a visual hand job on the digital dick using a smudge tool, represented by a finger-rubbing icon.

Some time ago I took part in a Kilroy programme to discuss what images women might enjoy. Coreen Sweet, a journalist who has worked for the Campaign Against Pornography and Censorship said on the programme 'erotica is fine ... but pornography is bad because it makes sexism sexy.' The idea that there is a safe distinction between erotica and pornography is a familiar tenet in the anti-pornography campaigns. To suggest that erotica is good, pornography bad is, in my opinion, just plain nonsense. If you find some pornography exciting, then it will be erotic for you. The erotic is a larger field than the pornographic, as objects termed erotic range from primitive sculpture to food to stockings. The pornographic on the other hand, as Linda Williams argues in her book *Hard Core*,[5] is a specific genre which has developed with the technology of photography as a tradition of representing the body's secret sexual pleasures. Williams suggests that the genre of pornography is a coincidence of 'visible frenzy'; the fascination of photographic truth, together with narratives of the bodily urge to confess sexual pleasure. It is a powerful combination which has so far been controlled by men. To say that 'pornography makes sexism sexy' is a clever media sound bite that means nothing. The sexism of the pornography industry is that it mainly represents women's sex for a male audience. This dynamic is not a result of pornography, it is much more than that, it is deeply embedded in our culture. The tradition of representing women as beautiful objects to be looked at by men, inflects a gendered division in the process of looking. When women interrupt this expectation they encounter more problems than might be expected. Power relations are disturbed that ordinarily help us to know who we are. I think this tension can be a radical addition to women's erotica. At the same time I do not want to underestimate the concerns that women have.

Coreen Sweet went on to say that as pornography was bad, what we really needed was 'something completely different'. I have called this article 'And now for something completely different' after her suggestion and I would like to think what this means in terms of making images. What is an image that is completely different? What is an erotic photograph that is completely different from others? Have you seen one? Would you be able to make one? How would you start? It is a daunting task. There is no such thing as a photograph that is completely different, that is at the same time recognisable. Photography is a signifying practice, a system of signs that is able to make meaning through the use of convention, reference and context. The plea for something different made by Sweet is understandable as women may not want the conventional meanings of pornogrpahy to be associated with their work, but at the same time it is very problematic for the woman artist. Modern art celebrates innovation and the Avant Garde, yet women artists past and present are persistently marginalised, within its framework. As we know from *Old Mistresses*[6] by Griselda Pollock and Roszika Parker the very idea of originality is itself a gendered domain.

In Simon Watney's book *Policing Desire*,[7] he clearly dismantles the visual/political theories at root in the anti-pornography campaigns. He goes on to suggest that we stop using the word pornography because of the moral discourse it inevitably describes. Many women feel strongly torn and caught up with what the word means for them. By getting rid of the term pornography we won't get rid of the problems associated with it. And these may be different to the problems Watney describes, as his concerns are to do with how pornographic material produced for gay markets is censored and regulated by the authorities. The situation is different for women whose traditional involvement in the sex industry is as dancers, actresses, models and sex workers. The idea that women could also be consumers or producers of pornography/erotica seems to run contrary not only to traditional models of femininity, but also to the building blocks of modern feminism. As Coreen Sweet said, 'pornography makes sexism sexy,' a statement that is only understandable in terms of how contemporary feminism informs our reading of the image. The challenge here is to loosen the knot of 'sexy sexism'. Without doing that we are back to the traditional split of good girls who are 'pure' and bad girls who are 'dirty' and let the side down.

At the end of the chapter on 'Pornography and AIDS', Watney

quotes a gay man in America as having said, 'to hate porn is to hate sex … porn tells us that sexuality is great, and in an age of AIDS that is an important message to hear.' At the time of reading, this stuck in my mind as something I could understand politically and yet made me feel very uneasy. The pornography that I had seen did not tell me that my sexuality was great. My feeling about pornography has been charged with rage and guilt. Rage at how women are depicted, guilt that the places I can look are supposed to be for gay/straight men. I have wanted to obliterate pornography because it does not include me as an active spectator, it does not address me and my visual pleasures. This overlaps with Watney's suggestion that we should avoid the term in debate. Avoidance is different from the wish to obliterate, which I have known, and I see as a recurrent theme in the feminist anti-pornography campaigns.

I started off my research for WSW cautiously envious of the way gay culture enjoys and creates erotica in a way which seems to be life affirming and relatively guilt free. Over the last few years I have met many women involved with issues of sexuality and visual practice. Lesbian artists/intellectuals have moved the debate on from arguments about the inescapable 'male' gaze, to a more interesting discussion of representing lesbian desire. Women working on images of men are also making inroads into the debate and are asking questions about how to represent or trace women's desire for a man. Most evident from my research for WSW, is that many women artists want to review the situation and discuss the issues of representing the man's sex.

Pornography is a cultural practice which has traditionally excluded women as spectators but has none the less depicted women's sexuality as avid and not reducible to the baby/marriage drive. As a genre, its basic idea is that sex is pleasurable and exciting, but not natural. In this sense it is an interesting area for women to explore, and think about again. We have hit upon a unique moment where the pornographic industry wants to capitalise on perceived new markets for women's pornography. Women photographers are central to the credibility of this new product. I am quite sure that if women artists do get involved then the work they produce will differ from existing pornography. But to concentrate on or to insist that women's work will be something completely different is to miss the point. The difference will be less visible; more out of frame. It will be about who is looking, who is making the images and whether these women will be allowed/will allow themselves to take their visual pleasure seriously.

Notes

[1] This article is based on one of the same name which appeared in *Variant* Issue 12 Summer/Fall 1992.

[2] The *What She Wants* exhibition opens at Impressions Gallery, York, on 18 September 1993 and will then tour Britain.

[3] For example, 'Why have there been no great women artists' Linda Nochlin in *Art and Sexual Politics*, Thomas B. Hess, Collier Books, New York, 1973.

[4] *What She Wants* is an experimental reversal of the dominant traditions of erotica in which man looks at woman, or male artists eroticise the body of the woman. WSW does not assume that the artists or viewers of the show are necessarily heterosexual.

[5] Linda Williams, *Hard Core: Power, Pleasure and the Frenzy of the Visible*, Pandora Press, London 1990.

[6] Griselda Pollock and Roszika Parker, *Old Mistresses: Women, Art and Ideology*, Routledge & Kegan Paul, London 1981.

[7] Simon Watney, *Policing Desire: Pornography, AIDS, and the Media*, University of Minnesota Press, Minneapolis 1987.

Penis Envy

NAOMI SALAMAN

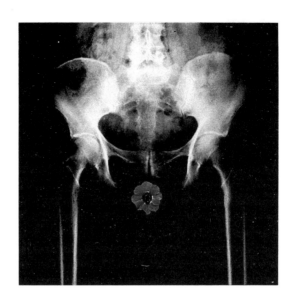

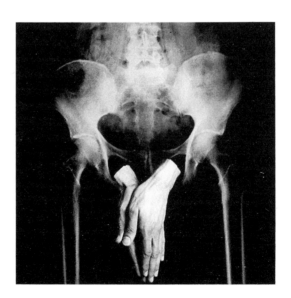

Penis Envy

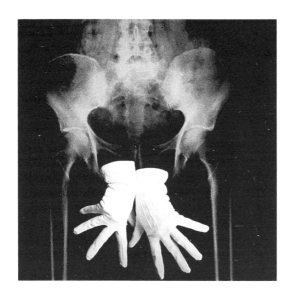

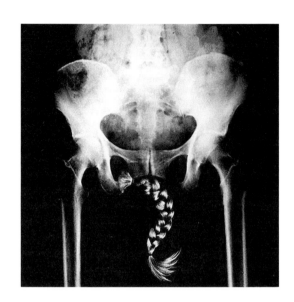

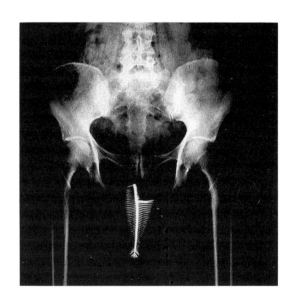

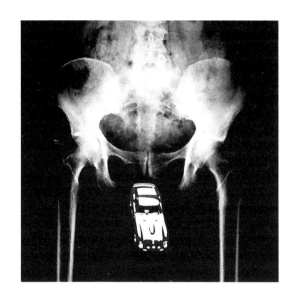

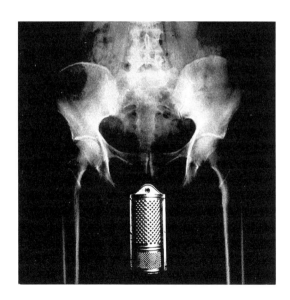

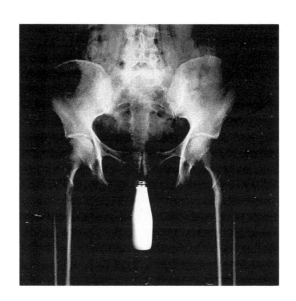

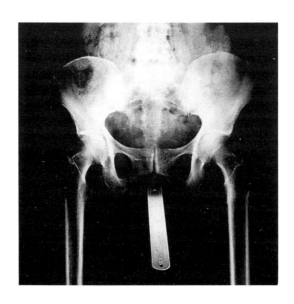

Penis Envy

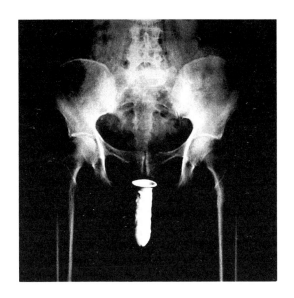

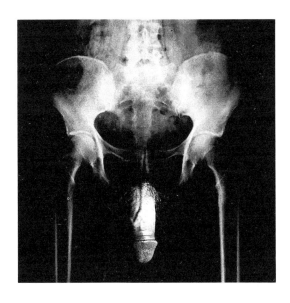

Distinguishing Looks: Masculinities, the Visual and Men's Magazines

SEAN NIXON

Introduction

In this chapter, I want to advance a series of arguments about the visual languages of masculinity that appeared in popular magazines for men in the mid-to-late 1980s. The representations I discuss here are tied in with the growth of men's general interest magazines in the UK.[1] These magazines – notably, *Arena, GQ,* and *Esquire* – are currently going from strength to strength in terms of circulation figures, but I have chosen to focus on the formative moment of these magazines in the UK for particular reasons. First, I want to insist that the images from this moment represent an important break in popular representations of masculinity. They do something decisively new. At root here is the marked ambivalence around the signs of maleness and the sanctioning of the display of narcissism. Second, I want to suggest that these visual representations underscore the importance of the places and practices of consumption in pluralising contemporary forms of manliness. The processes of marketing and selling – clothing, grooming products, de luxe goods, and accessories, in the case of these magazines – takes established forms of manliness and turns them so that you can't quite see them in the old terms again. At the heart of this process are visual pleasures and modes of looking. The magazines I discuss here establish ways of looking that pose questions about sexuality and sexual identity in relation to the masculinities they represent.

Central to this is the way the relationship between the male readers of the magazines and the models in the representations is established through the framing of forms of masculine-masculine looking. There is an intensity of the look at the male body. I argue in this chapter that these modes of looking and their associated codings of masculinity draw upon regimes of sexualized representation historically associated with gay men.

The third dimension to my interest in this period of representation is more autobiographical and political. The moment of the mid-to-late 1980s was a moment of optimism in terms of a popular politics of masculinity. It is a moment in which shifts in the visual iconographies of masculinity were receiving some sympathetic readings from a range of cultural critics. Frank Mort most lucidly attempted to set out the novelty of these new masculinities in popular representation and in young men's stylistic choices. Mort was optimistic that these shifts in public forms of masculinity could lay the basis for a new settlement of gender relations.[2] *Marxism Today* and the one day event 'Men, Breaking Out – A Sexual Politics for the 90s' (held in June 1987) were important in providing an institutional support for that politics.[3] Likewise, the conference *Body Politic/Erotic Self* belongs to this tradition.

My own work in this area is a product of this set of political interventions. I remember at the time (entering the third term of Thatcherism), the pleasurable perversity of a situation in which (at least as Mort argued) the market appeared to be throwing up some new 'progressive' masculinities. This politics of masculinity – rooted in arguments about taking popular culture seriously and in addressing the question of popular pleasures (at a time when most of the middle class left were still crushingly embarrassed about shopping at *Habitat*)[4] – offered the hope that the tide of history wasn't all moving away from the 'left' and the politics of the new social movements; that it was possible to identify with progressive currents in popular culture.

Returning to this moment of representation prompts a reconsideration of these political interventions. In retrospect it is easier to raise problems with them. Mort and Bennet – in different ways – have cogently argued for the shortcomings of this kind of Gramscian influenced cultural politics. Mort – in what is an implicit revision of his earlier intervention – talks about the 'instrumentalism' that informs this cultural politics and its 'continual slippage between the ambiguously specified areas of politics and culture' (Mort, 1992:29). Bennett has outlined in similar terms the way this model of cultural (and I would argue, sexual) politics commits us to 'too automatic a politics, one which – since it contends that all cultural activities are bound into a struggle for hegemony – is essentially the same no matter what the region of application' (Bennet, 1992:29). They both identify, then, the way these readings of popular culture tend and tended to instrumentally run a calculus through cultural forms as a precursor to some unspecified intervention: 'Is this cultural form progressive?' or 'Is it regressive?' for the projects of gender, sexual and social equality. The lesson of this mode of cultural politics – in relation to a politics of masculinity – is twofold: first, the importance of a 'politics of representation' necessitates a much fuller dialogue with those cultural practitioners involved in popular cultural production if an effective intervention is to be made; and second, a better sense is needed of the end that is being sought in intervening. In whose interests is a change in masculinity being made? In whose authority is the change being defined? These are not peripheral questions to the 'real' politics of refashioning dominant and exclusive forms of masculinity and heterosexuality. The representations I consider here continue to throw up, I think, the urgency of this problem of rethinking a sexual politics when it engages with the popular, and the very rationale of this engagement.

A final aspect of reconsidering this moment is more personal. In insisting on the importance of this moment of representation, there is a biographical thread at work here. This is the question of my own investment in these images. The masculine pleasures – around dress and grooming, including the possibility of an ambivalent sexual identification – that I suggest were opened up by some of the representations, were experienced by me at the time as positive developments; the coming into alignment of a new sense of self. Or, that at least is the story I tell myself about them. The reading of the representations that I set out here, then, marks a coming of age for me in relation to this moment of representation and the sexual/cultural politics that guided my initial interest in them.

Returning to this period of representation testifies to the fact that the heart too has its reasons.

Imaging Men in Men's magazines: 'Buffalo', 'Italianicity' and 'Edwardian Englishness'

The immediately striking feature of men's magazines by 1987/8 is the sheer volume of representations of masculinity. From advertisements for clothing, toiletries and alcohol, to 'people' portraits and the fashion spreads, the magazines are a bulging parade of masculinities shot, posed, lit and dressed in a number of ways. In straight quantitative terms, then, the emergence of the men's general interest magazine has produced a proliferation of representations of menswear and accessories; a proliferation that took-off from a very limited representational base.

In reading these representations, I want to highlight the pivotal role played by fashion stylists in shaping these visual languages. One stylist looms large in my account: the late Ray Petri. Petri enters our story as an occasional stylist for *The Face* magazine in 1983. By 1985, this former singer in a mid-60s 'R&B' band and rag trade hanger-on had established himself as the magazine's most distinctive stylist. Along with extra-curricular activities, like styling the members of Culture Club for the group's *Colour By Numbers* album, Petri's stylings established a distinctive masculine vocabulary under his 'Buffalo' trademark. These stylings exerted a strong if complicated influence over the imaging of masculinities within the fashion spreads of men's magazines as they emerged at the end of the 1980s (most strongly over *Arena*'s fashion) and a wider field of representation (notably in advertising).[5] What, though, was so distinctive about Petri's stylings?

'Buffalo' Boys

Petri produced regular fashion spreads for *The Face* between 1983 and 1987. He assembled a close group of models and associates. They formed his trademark 'Buffalo' boys (and girls). Along with photographer Jamie Morgan, 'Buffalo's' prominent faces included the models Nick and Barry Kamen and Zane. This was a 'family affair', as the headline to a fashion spread once put it. Casting, for Petri, was the essential element in constructing the 'Buffalo' 'look'.

'Buffalo' established some important innovations in what became termed 'street style'. Away from the established catwalks, Petri's stylings drew on and helped shape a distinctive repertoire of urban style. Most famously his styling of the MA-1 flight jacket turned the item into an essential element in 'tough', street style. Testifying to Petri's influence, *The Face*, in its review of 1989, suggested 'Who could argue that the combination of MA-1 flight jacket, Levis 501s and Dr. Martens is the urban uniform of the decade?' (*The Face*, vol , 100:50)

The fashion styled by Petri asserted a tough, muscular masculinity that drew tangentially on the representational genres of 1950s bodybuilding and boxing portraiture. In line with the ambiguous and ironic handling of a range of subject matter in *The Face*, 'Buffalo' knowingly played on a 'simpler' and fixed sense of masculinity. References to this pre-permissive manliness were spliced with the contemporary paraphernalia of style to carve out a striking and distinctive repertoire of codings of masculinity.

If we take an example from January 1985 ('Fashion Expo', *The Face*, 1985) the model chosen is young and physically well-built, with strong, hard features. Together these elements produce a mixture of boyish softness – connoted through the clear skin and the hat pushed back on the head – and an assertive maleness – connoted by his physical solidity. This combination of 'boyishness' and the solid body form represents one of a number of contradictory elements of masculinity held together in this image, and is typical of the 'Buffalo' stylings. This combination of elements produces some deliberately ambivalent significations around the signs of maleness. The ambivalence of 'soft' and 'hard' is reinforced by the casting of a light black model. This casting is important beyond its status as a signature element of 'Buffalo'. In terms of the signification of masculinity, two connotative 'moments' come into play: an equivalence of 'light black' with sensuality; and of 'black masculinity' with hyper-masculinity. The equivalence of 'black masculinity' with a hyper-masculinity is easiest to read. As a popular representational regime it has a long history, shaped by a pathologizing of blackness and is the site of pronounced fantasies about black men's sexuality

© Shoot that Tiger! Photo by Cindy Palmano

and physical prowess. These connotations of black masculinity operate as an important trace within the signification of the light-black male; they impart the connotations of an assertive masculinity. However, 'light black' has a partially separate set of connotations. The light black model makes possible the sanctioning of masculine sensuality. It does this through the indices of skintone and features. The casting of the light black model makes possible the playing off of 'soft' and 'hard'.

In the styling of the clothes in the 'Buffalo' spreads a recurrent allusion is to workwear: in this example it is the labourer's hat, the rolled up sleeves, and the heavy-duty cotton top. There is also a clear reference to the 'collage dressing' of punk style, in which various inappropriate objects and materials are assembled together; for example, the safety pin worn as accessory. The effect in this image, as it is in punk styles, is to disrupt established ways of dressing and to present the body as a surface on which objects and images can be plastered and hung. This styling draws attention to the construction of a 'look', to the process of 'bricolage'.[5]

The styling here emphasises the piling up of contradictory elements. In another 'Buffalo' plate ('Hard is the Graft', *The Face*, March 1985), an oversized jacket and hat, plastered with a newspaper headline style banner, are set off with a patterned silk tie and large encrusted earring. A range of accessories loom large in the stylings: US military tie-pins and more 'dressy' 'jewels, that rework male jewellery in a bricolage spirit. This is, on occasions, pushed to outrageous limits: the combination of jewelled bracelets and long black gloves worn with sportswear (vest top and track bottoms), signalling both 'masculinity' and 'femininity', 'physique' and 'elegance', in the same 'look'.

This assemblage of elements threw up a range of further combinations across the fashion Petri styled. Motorcycle boots were worn with trunks or lacey boxer shorts on muscular models, topped off with tank top and jacket. Dr Marten boots were mixed with a jumper and trunks replete with knuckle-duster. Less emphatically suits, ties and waistcoats were combined with both accessorising jewellery and also clumpy boots and sunglasses. Elements in this fashion drawn from US military style – the tie pins, the leather jacket, the Aviator 'raybans' and even, perhaps, the greased quiff –

testified to an 'American cool', and the pursuit of a 'more serious pose'.

Petri's 'Buffalo' fashion was resolutely, stylishly masculine. The accessories – and occasionally the revealed body – extended the conventional repertoire of menswear. This process represented a loosening of some fixed significations around masculinity: the styles were about a 'knowing', self-conscious sense of maleness that was pushed to the edges of camp. All of which was worked with the distinctive choice of models and recurrent kinds of grooming: cropped hair, sideburns, quiffs and hair boyishly brushed forward, glowing and shiny skins.

The posing and the models' expressions stood out in this fashion. Eyes, mouth, chin, nose and sometimes muscular arms and thighs were foregrounded, giving an intensity to the representations. The conventions of modelling were knowingly drawn upon, in order to attain the perfect pout and the moody stare. The use of conventions was often particularly marked, playing on the posture of an aggressive masculinity or parodying assertively masculine ways of standing. Across these images the postures and forms of expression gave a distinctive gloss to what we might call the romantic individuality of male youth. These were the street-wise, pretty, hard boys of popular mythology, from James Dean on. These romantic masculine identities offered resources for a 'tough', stylish masculinity – men who carried their maleness with a self-contained poise. A certain pre-permissive feel is important in accenting this masculine romanticism. This was brought into sharper focus in some of the 'Buffalo' images by the Kobal-esque finish to the black and white photographs. Glamour, evoked through the seamless surface of the photo, had a nostalgic edge here; polished gloss of 1940s and 50s film star portraiture applied to the art of 'lookin' good' in 80s street style. ('Hard is the Graft', *The Face*, 3/85)

The 'Buffalo' stylings are marked by the strongly narcissistic absorption and self-containment of the models. Posed usually alone, their gaze is often focused downwards or side-ways out of frame, registering self-reflection and (in certain spreads) a hint of melancholy. Part of this relates to 'Buffalo's' accenting of the tropes of male romanticism and individualism in terms that register the restrictions on young men in 80s 'Hard Times' culture (reduced life-chances, lack of money, the authoritarian shifts in social life).[6] More significantly, however, the conventions of posing and expression established in the spreads invite the viewer into complicitly or identification with the models' narcissistic absorption in his 'look' or self-presentation; complicity in the ways he carries his 'looks' and appearance.

What is important for my argument is the way this invited complicity in the model's narcissism is focused upon men's bodies that are at once highly masculine and openly sensual. Two aspects are crucial here. First, the attention staged upon the models appearance and the pleasure this establishes (in the quality and styling of the clothes, in his grooming, his 'looks', in the lighting and quality of the paper reproduction) are not directed towards an imagined feminine spectator who would triangulate the look between the male model and the imagined male viewer. That is, there are no women in the representation or implicitly addressed by the staging of the image to encode this masculine-masculine look as normatively heterosexual. Secondly, the choice of the models and some of the elements of clothing in the stylings have a strong intertextuality with certain traditions of representation of masculinity aimed at and taken up by gay men; notably the valorizing of a 'tough' masculinity. The *Palmano Man* calendar for 1987 produced a particularly explicit example of this intertextuality. Advertised in gay magazines like *Square Peg*, and featuring 'thirteen classic male images ... the perfect present for someone special', the calendar was styled by Petri and featured black and white men shot in three-quarter length shots displaying muscular arms, chest and shoulders in vest tops and chunky accessories.

I am not suggesting, however, that the 'Buffalo' codings were gay male codings; or that they were straightforwardly that. There was a limited displaying of the surface of the body in the fashion spreads and the choice of models broke with the tighter generic figures of some more explicitly sexualised gay representations (such as the denim clad boy or the cop), 'Buffalo' was strongly rooted in the stylistic community that it both invoked and simultaneously represented, and this was not stricly defined in terms of sexuality. What is pivotal, however, is the way the styling organised a masculine-masculine look that drew upon a gay index without pathologising that index or resolving the tension set up in the ambiguity of the gay/straight image.

Classics go Latin

A play on what I call 'Italianicity' occurred in both *Arena* and *GQ* in the period between 1986–9. In describing the representations, I use the term to refer to the 'condensed essences of a mythical Italian masculinity.[7] The casting of the models is important in establishing these connotations of 'Italianicity'. These are often anchored by written headlines such as 'Roma', (*Arena* number 16) 'Latin Groves' (*Arena* number 13).

A particular index of skin tone, strong features and a marked sensuality (the lips, particularly are pronounced) is prominent. As with the 'Buffalo' stylings these elements signify both sensuality and hardness, a mixture of both 'soft' and 'hard'. The casting of 'Italian' models within these spreads produces a set of connotations of masculinity similar to those signified by the casting of light-black models. 'Italianicity' provides a rich pool from which to build up these connotations. The physiognomy of the models is comple-mented by allusions to the bravado and swagger of an 'Italian' macho – an appeal to 'Roman' pride and passion. A spread titled 'After Dark' emphatically plays on the connotations of this register of 'Italianicity'. A strong element of the spread is the theme of the gang, drawing on the staging of rituals of aggression and display: stylized bravado, stares, pouts and tensed bodies, evoke the frisson of controlled confrontation in the city at night.

The location setting is important in connoting 'Italianicity'. Often we find narrow streets with pitted, worn walls and arches; iron-worked balconies; window shutters; lace curtains and palms as the backdrop to the stylings. All of which adds to the sense of drama and atmosphere. The location setting of the Tuscany region, for example, is used as the immediate context for the fashion in one spread. Either amongst the 'Chianti Fields of Green', or 'Latin Groves', the countryside appears to mirror the quality of the clothes: the lush fields and Tuscany light play off the cool wool suits and cotton. This, of course, is a different kind of Italy to that evoked in 'After Dark' where, as I have indicated, the Northern city provides

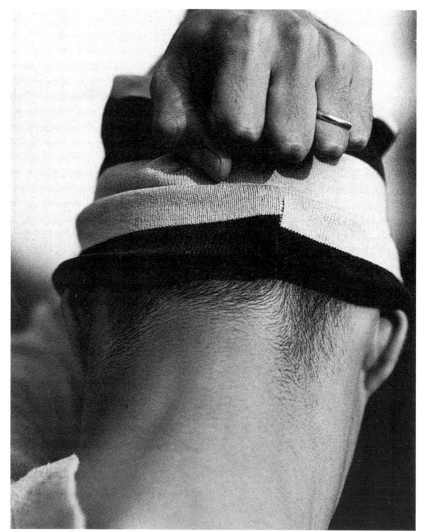

This is a rock solid body regime 'sculpted from stone'...
Angelo Valentino, *Arena*

the backdrop to the invocation of prowling gangs.

The clothes styled in the spreads reinforce the sense of 'Italianicity'. A central element to this is the bravado of the styles: generously cut suits are worn with trashy, 'bad taste' ties and silver shirts, finished off with flashy dark glasses; 'swanky' white suits, embroidered shirts and panama hats are lined up, together with wide profiled overcoats and jackets. These are big and bold clothes that emphasise and accentuate the masculine frame.

The assertive masculinity of the styles is carried through in much of the posing of the models. As with the 'After Dark' spread. 'Dateline Milan' works with a similar regime of gesture and expression: moody stares, and upright poses. This is a rock-solid bodily regime, 'sculpted from stone', as a caption puts it. As we've seen before with 'Buffalo', the body in these spreads is foregrounded, playing up its physicality. These spreads draw on well established masculine codings: the upward focused stares; a gaze that is sideways and away from the imagined viewer.[8] Or a narcissistically absorbed look.[8]

One spread gives a particular twist to this narcissism: lost to his 'sweet (day) dreams of youth', the model's relaxed pose is enhanced by the casual clothes, and particularly by the boxer shorts that loosely frame his thighs. A look is established here that draws the eye to the cusp of the clothing – leg. As if to register this look and disperse the frisson of its sexual connotations for the imagined male viewer, a wall-hung photograph of a woman (perhaps the subject of his 'sweet dreams'?) mediates between the reader and the model. She triangulates the relation between the reader and male model within the terms of normative heterosexual relations. That is, the picture stitches the look invited at his bared thighs into a display that is primarily directed at the woman.

However, the smallness of the photograph, its marginality in the frame, and the way the model's attention in the narrative of the plate is not upon the photograph, leave his relation to her as open and ambiguous. They suggest another kind of sexualisation of the look is also possible. Other spreads – in *Arena* particularly – construct heterosexual relations that are not so much normative as problematic. At times the posings of male and female models code heterosexuality as an 'impossible relation': the models are disconnected from each other by gender, unable to engage either by eye contact or by the intimacy of physical proximity.

'How Very English': 'Edwardian Englishness'

An invocation of what I have called 'Edwardian Englishness' provides the third figure that looms large in the spreads. These images present a particular version of Englishness: the pale white skin and the distinctive haircuts – cropped at the sides and back with the top left long enough to be pushed back with sweeping hand movements, and slightly weighted down with hair grease though free to flop forward. There is still the playing off of 'soft' and 'hard'. But this is not as pronounced as in the 'Buffalo' and 'Italianicity' stylings. What is distinctive, however, is the repertoire of clothing worn. Plundering a casually formal wardrobe, the emphasis is on linens and cottons in white, pastels and 'country' colours. In one spread, for example, white linens are worn with paisley cravat; and taupe, cream and beige jackets and trousers are set off with silk ties, cravats and waistcoats in green and red. The choice of cut and fabrics evokes a colonial, aristocratic, Englishness.

These connotations are further underlined by the selection of materials for the sets and props. In one spread, 'Colony Club', the clothing styles are glossed as the 'Englishman abroad – literally down at the (Colony) Club. Embroidered 'oriental' rugs, cane chairs and a wicker work elephant are some of the important signifiers in this particular set of images. Alternatively, the English countryside forms an evocative backdrop to the fashion: the wind blown spring skies and flat, sandy coastlines connote a 'temperate isle' Englishness.

Ways of standing and looking animate the styles and settings. The 'Colony Club's' aura as an exclusively masculine domain is connoted in the posing of the models. The formality and stiffness of these poses signifies the appropriate indices of class and power, while the social context of the club is confirmed by the grouped posing. The models pose square on and upright. This is complemented by arrogant and assertive stares to camera. Sometimes a more languid regime of posture and expression is staged: models sit astride a breakwater, piling up sand with their hands or wistfully contemplating the oncoming tide.

66

The textual devices of lighting, cropping and developing, establish a further set of meanings across the spreads. Colour, tinting and lighting crucially assert, in a number of the images, the connotations of 'Edwardian Englishness'. The sense of early evening light developed in the spreads is soft, languid and 'deep'. It is evocative of a version of Englishness' imagined in terms of salty coastlines, spring showers and a distinctive quality of light. A further twist on this is found in 'Colony Club'. Here the grainy, amber lighting signals 'golden days'. The image is infused with a sense of the warm, rich and fading light of a fondly remembered past. This is the dying, late afternoon sunlight of the 'dreaming spires' of Oxbridge.

The physiognomy of the models, the clothes, props and lighting – invoke an established repertoire of 'Englishness'. I have in mind here, most notably, the 'Raj genre' of films, together with Merchant and Ivory's highly successful films of Forster's novels, as well as Granada TV's 'classic' adaptation of Waugh's *Brideshead Revisited* that spoke so powerfully to the popular imagination through the 1980s (and undoubtedly continue to do so). The success of these films came in part through their emphatic reproduction of colonial, Edwardian England through costume and sets. The 'look' of the films was a central part of their appeal. In 'Brideshead Revisited', for example, it was Jeremy Irons looking dashing in period costume against the backdrop of the splendour of Castle Howard that was as important as the prestigious literary adaptation.

There is a further dimension to this appeal to 'Edwardian Englishness'. The invocation and (inevitable) reworking of this repertoire of 'Englishness' signified powerfully in the context of 80's Britain through the Thatcherite rhetoric of 'little Englandism'. The reproduction of a narrowly based version of Englishness – and English masculinity – is a feature of the spreads.[9] However, as some of the films mentioned above testify, there are connotations of 'sexual abberations' associated with this aristocratic Englishness. A specific ethnicity is underscored by its articulation with homosexuality or at least sexual ambivalence. This hinted-at sexuality manifests itself in the spreads through the slightly self-conscious use of the conventions of posing; that is, the signifying of a stylized, almost aestheticised sense of identity. The form of the masculine-masculine look in these spreads, then, is staged in terms of an identification with the model; an identification with the power of his imagined Englishness, as well as in the less clearly articulated forms of sexuality.

Conclusion

What have these accounts of the fashion spreads delivered? I have picked out three important figures – 'Buffalo', 'Italianicity' and 'Edwardian Englishness'. They are by no means the only figures I could have chosen. In themselves, though, they demonstrate that there were a number of versions of the 'new man' on offer even within the limited field of representation of the magazines. In my accounts of the spreads I have been concerned to emphasise the organisation of spectatorship and its interlinking with the codings of masculinity.

I do, however, want to insist on the importance of the kinds of ambivalent masculine-masculine looking framed in the 'Buffalo' stylings in particular. It is the way 'Buffalo' set up pleasures in looking that draw on forms of looking, historically the prerogative of gay men, without pathologising that look, or attempting to reinscribe a violent hierarchy between gay and straight by resolving the ambivalence of that look, that makes them so distinctive. In the context of the developments in men's magazines in the last couple of years and, to some extent, the assertion of a more entrenched articulation of difference around the category of 'Queer' by a new generation of gay/queer men, the space 'Buffalo' established for an assertive ambivalence within visual languages of masculinities has faded.

Is there anything left to say, then, about the codings and the shifts in modes of spectatorship that I have charted in the spreads from the mid-to-late 1980s? Do they have anything to tell us about the cultures of masculinity on the ground in that period – in particular the gender scripts of the consumers of the magazines (and the visual regimes that drew upon them)? Did these modes of spectatorship have any effects on these lived cultures, and do they have any ongoing significance?

It would be dangerous to imply too much from a formal reading of visual texts about the kinds of subjective investments made by 'real' readers in the looks estalished in the plates. Piecing together a picture of the actual investments made by readers (in the historical context of their reading) would require a subtle reconstruction of the moment of reading or viewing. In particular we would need to know more about the ways the looks formally established in the magazines were assimilated into everyday practices: the effects of the activity of reading or glancing through the magazines themselves; the social relations that shaped that reading; the related activities of shopping and looking for clothes and grooming products; and the relation of these looks to other 'languages of looking'.

As I suggested at the outset, however, the spreads do point to the importance of the institutional spaces of consumption (in this case popular magazines) in pluralising the masculine scripts available to men. In this sense, the magazines I have discussed here are shaped within a longer cultural history of post-war pop culture and consumption. This is a history that has thrown up a specific set of masculinities – most spectacularly within mod subculture in the mid-60s, soul boys and Bowie boys in the 1970s, and the experimentations of 'Blitz Culture' in the early 1980s. These masculinities have been in some kind of critical relation to the mainstream culture's narratives and conventions of a normative heterosexual masculinity – specifically in terms of the space they represented for sexual ambiguity and homosexualities. How we begin to unravel the impact of the visual languages I have charted (and the moment out of which they come) upon popular masculinities on the ground, needs to be sensitive to their uneven unfolding (including, importantly their outright failure to address certain masculinities) and needs to locate them within a history of post-war masculinities.

Notes

[1] In this chapter I am focusing primarily on *Arena* (Wagadon) launched in November 1986; and *GQ* (Condé Nast) launched in November 1988. The men's general interest magazine sector currently also includes, *Esquire* (National Magazines) launched in January 1991; and *FHM* (C.J. Astridge IV) launched in 1985 (initially through retail outlets as *For Him*).

[2] Frank Mort 'Boy's Own: Masculinity, Style and Popular Culture', in *Male Order, Unwrapping Masculinity* (ed) R. Chapman and J. Rutherford (Lawrence & Wishart, London 1988).

[3] A selection of contributions to this event appeared in *Male Order, ibid.*

[4] On consumption and left politics see, for example: Stuart Hall 'The Culture Gap' in *Marxism Today* (January 1984); Fredric Jameson 'Pleasure: A Political Issue', in *Formations of Pleasure* (RKP, London 1983).

[5] See, for example, Iain Chambers *Popular Culture – the Metropolitan Experience* (Methuen, London 1986).

[6] These comments on 'Hard Times' masculinity draw on Janice Winship's argument in 'Back to the Future', in *New Socialist* no.40 1986.

[7] The notion of 'Italianicity' as the 'condensed essence' of Italianness is appropriated from Roland Barthes 'The Rhetoric of the Image', in *Image Music Text* (ed) S. Heath (Fontana, London 1977)

[8] On masculinity and representational conventions see, Richard Dyer 'Don't Look Now, The Instabilities of the Male Pin-Up', in *Screen* no.23 (1982).

[9] On the notion of 'Little Englandism', see Stuart Hall *The Hard Road to Renewal* (Verso, London 1988). On 'Raj Revival' films see, Kobena Mercer 'Recoding Narratives of Race and Nation', in *Black Film, British Cinema* (ed) K. Mercer (ICA Document 7, London, 1988).

Further reading
Bennett, Tony (1992) 'Putting Policy into Cultural Studies', in *Cultural Studies* (ed) Grossberg, L. Nelson, C. and Triechler, P. (Routledge, London 1992).
Mort, Frank (1992) 'Consumer Cultures, Political Discourses and the Problem of Cultural Politics', paper presented at the 'Theory, Culture and Society' Conference, University of Pittsburgh, USA.

Thanks to David Oswell for helpful comments.

Other Lovers

JACKIE KAY

This collection needed a poet to speak of love, as poetry gets beyond theory and politics travelling to the heartlands of desire, loss, jealousy and tenderness. These poems are parts of our interior lives. They recognise the limitations of our rational polemic about desire – a bridge to feeling behind the rhetoric.

Victoria

Other Lovers

You tell me the same story three or four times
and you know it's always going to vary a bit,
but what interests me is how I pretend
I have never heard it. It's always jealousy.

This time I'm sitting on the hard chair
and there is this upholstered throat,
and I know it now; I can't speak.
Pins all the way up from the apple.

And your eyes are shining and tremendous.
What's the matter – For some stupid reason
there's small fingers the size of ants
in there now as well. Under the floor boards.

It was the attic before; her in black lycra.
This time, all of a sudden, she's got on
gold sandals and fuck all else,
and you are, I know you are, still in love with her.

And I am, I know I am, mad as hell.
She was always going to get done.
Something is crawling along my jaw.
She is swearing you say swearing

like a trooper, like a company director.
That line is the same in all nine stories.
She never thought it'd be such a heavy sentence.
I'm the one serving a sentence; guarding my tongue.

I know when you get the taxi-bus from the station
to the prison in the country, you wear
dark glasses and always freshen up your lipstick
just before you give the same driver £1.50.

72

Other Lovers

You dress like dynamite. You wear things
you don't wear for me: the yellow sandals,
are in the plastic bag – you are vulnerable
trying to put them on, standing up, losing

your balance. You throw your head to laugh,
What's wrong? Darling, don't be so unreal.
She's inside. We both repeat ourselves.
How many times? I haven't said anything.

The Crossing

That evening, walking across the bridge,
the light drowning in the river,
the dark water wringing its hands,
till the bridge moved too, that evening.

And you, were not there.
So suddenly, in that dark place, I felt myself
go to you; as if I was two and one of me
went to you.

The bed, a boat on a dangerous crossing.
Neither of us knew where we were going.

II

I am crossing the same bridge alone.
Underneath it is dark and fast, the river.
I can't see myself. Lights hang on trees
by the banks – glowing and forbidden.

Dropping like fruit into the dark water.
Only to rise again.

No matter how many times we try to sink
our past – old bundles of clothes in the river –
a body surfaces

so suddenly, covered in wreaths. You are not there.
But someday you might go back. Love is light and dark.

III

I am trying to find the same small room.
Perhaps you might be in it, waiting.
Would you take me in,
Whisper the talk of the river, the babble tongue?

74

Other Lovers

Having all leads to nothing. There's the bundle
of past going down the river where one bank
becomes another. Now you have gone back to her.
I am here, crossing over, going back home.

Now it is my turn to miss, to look in the river.

This Long Night

This long night talks to itself.
The dark won't listen to the sound of your name.
I reach out here – my big empty bed.
The space next to me closes in; you say something,
anything, the exact sound of your accent
falling like rain on a caravan roof.
Tell me what you want me to do.

This long night stretches into another time.
Nobody calls my name. Silence –
a thief in the back garden.
Your body, a shadow, flat under the moon.
In my sleep, I open up like a night flower.
My scent comes in the midnight hour.
You come in by the window, don't you?

This long night and I can't reach you.
Your tongue inside me slides away.
You walk till the night grabs you.
A lonely pitch at the dark. Walk
until the road is all of your past.
Then, turn in your sleep next to your marriage,
wake yourself up calling my name.

The Keeper

Nowadays there are too many things to hide.
I am a keeper. Secrets are my caged animals.
I feed them things. Things they will like.
Each day a ritual; I keep time – though

there are days when I wish I could say,
to Hell; and watch the entire city run
riot with hippopotamus and rhinoceros
A city gent, an autobank, an elephant.

She has told me not to tell anyone.
I don't. These lies are fun. I'm good at them.
Not since I said my brother drowned
have I told such a whopper. One lie

leads to another: a zebra on the escalator.
One afternoon in a hotel room.
Where have you been? I lie again.
I play it all back, alone. Pause

on your face against a stranger's sheets.
There's a monkey swinging on Waterloo bridge.
Your face high up, till I pull you down.
London bridge is falling down, falling down.

I am losing it. I count time on fingers.
Another hour when I can't see straight.
The zebra's coming down with no stripes.
Somebody's messed with the zebra's stripes.

I wake to the sound of your voice
moving around my hollow head, my empty house.
I imagine your house. What colour are the walls?
The sheets? You and she, asleep between them.

Pleasure Principles

Are they stripes? I imagine you in this bed.
Here, my home. Nobody knows: I behave oddly.
Both the lions stayed apparently.
I thought that awful funny –

cage wide open. Soon it will out;
the truth always does. What will I do then?
Capture them in a net of lies.
One day I will keep things from you.

Dusting The Phone

I am spending my time imagining the worst that could happen.
I know this isn't a good idea, and that being in love I could be
spending my time going over the best that has been happening.

The phone rings heralding some disaster. Sirens.
Or it doesn't ring which also means disaster. Sirens.
In which case, who would ring me to tell? Nobody knows.

Loving you sweetheart right now is terrifying:
someone climbing through your window at nightime.
But also, a speedboat crossing the Aegean sea.

The future is a long gloved hand. An empty cup.
A marriage. A packed house. One night per week
in a stranger's sheets. Forget tomorrow.

You say, don't mention love. I try. It doesn't work.
I assault the postman for a letter, or
I go over and over our times together, re read them.

This very second I am waiting on the phone.
I polish it. I'll do it favours in return for your call
It has a personality. Infuriatingly

It sends me hoaxs, calls from boring people;
your imaginary hello sinks softer than sheets.
I am going to have to do something.

I am trapped in it. I can't move. I want you.
all the time. This is awful – a photo for company.
Come on, damn you, ring me. Or else. What?

I don't know what.

Sexual Manners

SUE GOLDING

I once picked up this woman – I won't tell you where, lest one of my favourite hunting grounds be overrun by voyeur pickers and not enough real fruit. It was late ... very late at night. I was wearing, and this is important: black-leather-in-the-extreme ('butch' but not quite 'daddy mode', as they say), with the usual assortment of toys – like hand-cuffs and rope (you know, things like that) hanging off the left side – indicating to anyone who might need or want indicating (anyone, I mean to say, already 'in the know' who wanted to know more) that they were in the presence of a rather *hungry* 'dom', a 'top', or in a word longer than three letters, a 'Master'. And in this particular case, on this particular night, it meant also that I was cruising for a specific kind of tit-bit, a real specific and rather juicy gourmet delight, in the form of an eager 'apprentice' (one could say, perhaps) an aggressive 'bottom' – someone who might be dressed, as I often like my playmates to dress, in whore-fem gear, trashy red lipstick, stilettoes and all.

Now, before I go on and tell you what happened, let me just say that these words: dom, Master, bottom, whore-fem, butch, Daddy-boy, cruising, play, play-mate, and so on, have their place. Or rather, they take a place and make a place. They make an impossible place take place. They describe, circumscribe, inscribe a spectacular space, a spectacle of space: an invented, made-up, unreal, larger-than-life-and-certainly-more-interesting space that people like myself sniff out and crave and live in and want to call 'Home'; a home I want to suggest that is entirely Urban; an urbanness I want to say that is entirely City and not at all – or at least not exactly – Community; a queer (kind of) city (or better yet, cities), that finally, not only privileges the Joke but has something to do with the cry: 'Freedom' …

But here I am getting ahead of myself, interrupting myself – though interruptions, have their place (don't you think?) indicating precisely what it is that they are not and therewith, doing the impossible; to wit, setting an agenda without setting it, mapping the map without mapping it directly, at any rate. But I digress.

It was late at night and dark, but not so dark that I could not spot 100 metres off exactly what it was I was looking for. Like a divining rod seeking – and finding – the divine, she was spot on. I strode over with a deliberate gait; she stood there, waiting, as if she knew already in advance the whole of the discussion about to take place. Two strides away, I called over to her with a remark not overly clever, and certainly not profound, something like, 'Nice outfit.' And she responded with something equally not clever nor profound; something like, 'Well, if you're into this, you'll certainly like what's underneath.' And I said, 'You into rough sex?' And she said, 'Your place or mine?' And I said, 'My car's right over there.' And she said, 'So, let's get the hell out of here.'

A playful, though fairly uncomplicated script – and I laughed to myself at the pleasure of it all; at the sheer audacity of seeking and finding, and getting at and getting beyond or, put better, of risking, the mundane. We left. Together. At that precise moment I remember thinking very clearly two things: first, that this was the smoothest, fastest, pick-up I had made in some time, especially given the fact that we actually *spoke* to each other – words often being useless where a possible consummation of sex is concerned; and second, that I *so much* preferred the artifice of surface (verbal or otherwise) to the sanctity of the profound.

Now, as it turned out, things went quite otherwise than expected – rope, rough sex, and inexperienced little calves being what they are – for when it came down to it, when the moment was nigh, when the apartment was ready for 'serious enquiries only'; that is, when we got to my place amidst all the well placed toys and lube and candle-lights (set there previous to my having gone out, with the sole intention of bringing someone, unknown, home to fuck); when, that is to say, she took off in a mad gallop through my tiny apartment; when, finally, thinking to myself 'this must be some sort of strange game of tag', so I played along; when eventually, sweating *solely* from the chase and not at all from the anticipation, I tackled her (less than suave, I must admit); when, despite the kind of fako-fako wrestling match that occurred, I roped her not unlike a calf in a rodeo, with the major exception that the knots were safety knots and could be undone in one pull if required; when, after turning away to light a cigarette, only to look back again and see her standing there, holding the rope in hand and smiling triumphantly, exclaiming: 'Yeah! I won!!'; when I then asked her 'But what precisely have you won?!'', and she responded, 'The game of Rough Sex' and when I responded: 'But WE HAVE NOT EVEN HAD SEX, LET ALONE ROUGH SEX'; and when all forlorn, she sat there pouting, her roped trophy sagging around her fingers; when I finally was compelled to ask her 'How old are you, anyway?' and she replied, 'Old enough' and I replied, 'Yes, old enough to get into a taxi and go on home, *alone*,' I realized right there and then just how complex this game of sexual manners (or as Foucault would call it, the 'problem of fishing around') can get. For the codes of the sexual are both self-evident and completely hidden exactly at the same time, though often for very different reasons, if one is gay or straight or transsexual or transvestite or a drag queen or a motorcycle mama or a prostitute or a daddy-boy or a madonna or a clone or all of the above or none of them.

Sexual manners. I'm sorry if the next remark will disappoint you, but this is not going to be a 'how to' primer on how to behave, i.e., on how one *must* behave sexually in order to be considered, by yourself or anyone else, perverse. (Though to be honest, I do most assuredly have a few practical tips on that subject – which I will most certainly share with you when I get to the sordid problem – or perhaps it is a solution? – of this oddly necessary thing called Gossip.) But, I digress, yet again. So, to get back to the immediate question of the sexual and the mannered and the queer little problem of fishing around, and what it is that I am *Not* going to do. Not only will I not attempt a 'how to behave' primer on the subject of fucking, neither will I attempt to distract attention and go off to try and dissect 'why' people might choose to behave in the incredibly diverse manner or manners they seem to take on at every turn. For both these 'how' and 'why' analyses, tend to bring with them, though in different ways what I call, the Trojan Horse Dilemma.

For the 'how' question (as in 'how to act'), often (not always, but often) brings with it a whole series of (eventually) rigid moralities to which one is *thereby EXPECTED TO*, nay, *COMPELLED TO*, aspire in the name of all that is or could be 'Good' or anyway, avant-garde. It is a privileging of capital 'E' Experience, as if it were totally objective – 'just the facts, ma'am' – and therewith able, worse yet, to yield one solid and proper way to behave in or around, this entity called real life; as if, there was one single, opaque, graspable, REALITY or *THING*, (for example called S&M or Vanilla sex or Lesbianism or Homosexuality or even Heterosexuality, for god's sake) and armed with the horizon of an objective truth, make it seem as though all one would then have to do simply would be to search for the exact, indeed *Polite Experience* of, in this case, sexuality in all its maddening flavours. But in the end, this kind of 'how to', really always and only creates *Puritanical Little Conformists*, avant-garde, S&M, vanilla, drag or otherwise.

On the other hand, and in the latter case, by posing the 'why question' – i.e., 'why' do people have the kind of sexual manners they have?, one can only, it would seem in the end, resuscitate in various and sundry ways the old bug-bear of essentialism, pure and simple. For the 'why' question asks, in effect: 'who are you that makes *you* want to do this or that?; why are you who you are? it insists you account for yourself as a self-accounting, actor in the world. And in the same breath as asking the question: what makes you do what it is you do? – like wanting to play with little girls, when the rest of the world wants you to play with little boys as a normal state of affairs – in the same breath as asking the question, it says, in effect: there *must* be the capital 'R' Reason for acting thus and so. And then, in order to capture the entirety of that Reason, the 'why' question propels us to search for the answer; that is, compels us to go off and find an objective, point-for-point First Cause for the condition of its emergence. This condition is often understood to emanate from God, but these days now also (indeed, usually) it is linked to some stupid notion of a 'general' (and always binarily gendered) human nature. Girls wear pink and boys wear blue and that is because 'girls will be girls' (sweet, nurturing and flower-like) and 'boys will be boys' (sweaty, aggressive, and animal-like) and if the girls wear blue and the boys pink, then that is because the girls must be boys and the boys must be girls. And if the girls must be boys, then they are probably dykes; and if the boys must be girls, then they are probably fags (which makes one wonder with whom they are having sex if the girls that the boyish-girls are fucking are into pink and the boys that the girlish-boys are fucking are into blue and so forth). Yes, I think you can see in what way the 'why' question tries one's patience to the extreme. It points to answers far too pure and simple. Ad nauseam.

And I have no doubt that you can come up with your own pathetic examples that you, too, have had to draw upon during some horrible luncheon, i.e., whenever you have gotten suckered into having to answer questions like 'why are you behaving like *THAT*?; why are you gay?; why must you dress in drag?; why are you a clone?' For the why question of *sexual* conduct, let alone, sexual style, often is reduced to some abstract notion of the maleness or femaleness of the genitalia – as if, in-searching between one's legs, the 'answer' would at once shout forth: pink! or blue! and everyone would know exactly what the hell that might imply in terms of actual physical fucking, and whether or not this meant you were queer, in terms of pleasures and practices. Endlessly, for all eternity, without ever being able to say, in the answer, that now, right now, the kind of sexual manners that exists are, indeed, in some crucial way, very *Different* from what they were *Before*, and that, having dropped this little bomb in the middle of my exegesis on 'whyness', that that very difference allows for the invention of a whole new ball game, around sex, and pleasure; indeed, life itself. But here, I am getting ahead of myself, speaking so candidly to you about inventions and difference, all in the name of manners and sex.

In short, these twin problems of 'the how to' and 'the why' of sexual comportment and its resulting moral codes, usually do no better than to take as a given what it is they are trying to prove, and then make us live up to it, to boot; or get mad at us if we don't; or think there is some deep psychological capital 'R' Reason if we do some of it most of the time and none of it the rest. There seems to be no room for the Cindy's of the world, who proclaimed on every banal radio station in the mid-80's: 'Girls –' and I mean by girls, men, women and anyone in between regardless of race, religion, sexual orientation, or employment status '– Girls just wanna have fun.' Rather, the Trojan Horse Dilemma adherents seem to take as a given that there is something 'out there' to be proved. And then, by golly, they go off and prove it ...

And because I want to torture you ever so slightly before I go on to some of the more juicy bits of sexual manners; or, to put it slightly differently, because I want to make sure that this point is clear to all you out there who might hear it better if it is put directly into a more philosophical language, let us, briefly, take note of our friend Ludwig Wittgenstein, and his rather brilliant remarks on the problems of privileging experience or searching for an ultimate ground; i.e., the 'how to/why' Trojan Horse Dilemma. He puts it like this:

> 125. If a blind man were to ask me 'Have you got two hands?' I should not make sure by looking. If I were to have any doubt of it, then I don't know why I should trust my eyes. For why shouldn't I test my *eyes* by looking to find out whether I see my two hands? *What* is to be tested by *what*? ...

> 130. But isn't it experience that teaches us to judge like *this*, that is to say, that it is correct to judge like this? But how does experience *teach* us, then? [he asks]. *We* may derive it from experience, but experience does not direct us to derive anything from experience. If it is the *ground* of our judging like this, and just the cause, still we do not have a ground for seeing this in turn as a ground.

> 131. No, experience is not the ground for our game of judging. Nor is it its outstanding success.

> 140. We do not learn the practice of making empirical judgments by learning rules: we are taught *judgments* and their connexion with other judgments. A *totality* of judgments is made plausible to us.[2]

Judgments are political in the most prurient sense of the term. What becomes the grist for our accessing what must be (i.e., both the 'is' and the 'ought'), and in so accessing, what must become part and parcel of various judgments themselves. That accessing, not to mention the very construction of the judgment itself, is precisely, and always, a political struggle. A hegemonic one, as Gramsci would say. Establishing, a 'nodal point', a bubbling cauldron of sorts, like the core of a star, boiling and ruptured and fractured, but core, nonetheless; core without posing boundaries; core without posing rigid 'truths', but creating them anyway; creating 'truths', fractured and burning and dangerous and able to be melted, nonetheless.

Ok. So it is like this, then: if *Experience* cannot give us a basis for the judgement, and if, on the other hand, we do not have some overall objective *Truth* to ground the truth, how the hell do we know the whole truth and nothing but the truth so help us God? How do we know when we're right? And not only that, but how do we know the actual rules of the game, any game, sexual or otherwise? How do we know they are 'real'?; how do we know they are *Ethical*?

The short answer, I'd say, is that: we don't. The longer answer is: Ahhh, but we do, Blanch, we do.

Wittgenstein puts it like this: that the rule itself is grounded in the way in which it is *used*; that is to say, in its 'technique', and more than that, in the 'physical and psychological facts that make the technique *possible*.'[3] The 'wherefore art thou, oh rule' as if a first-cause or a 'how to' or an end – in-itself, or as something that says 'this and this *will be* the outcome *because* that and that is the case', is left entirely out of his picture. 'When I say,' says Wittgenstein, ' "If you follow the rule this *must* come out", that doesn't mean: it must, because it always has. Rather, that it comes out – is one of my *foundations*.'[4]

You see, in this example, the 'ground' of truth, as it were, is neither an 'x' nor a 'not-x'; that is to say, it is neither an already given, fully formed Being or its opposite, a not-already given, fully formed Being; nor is it a constructed kind of not-Being nor the opposite of that weird little entity, i.e., not-constructed, not fully formed Being) ... or any other combination of Being you can think of: Woman is NOT the complete difference of Man; Heterosexuality is NOT the complete difference of Lesbianism: rather, Lesbianism, or Heterosexuality, or whatever are *application* (technique), in the most impure and profane sense of the terms, 'through which we *grasp*,' says Ludwig, 'a regularity'.[5] That is, says Sue Golding, a 'route', a mapping, an impossible geography – impossible not because it does not exist, but because *it exists and does not exist exactly at the same time*. And here, if I wanted to be really cruel, I would launch into a digression on quantum physics and the importance of relativity, the role of things called technological space-time, space as time, or even whole digressions around quasi-somethings we can call, hauntingly enough, 'The Elsewhere'. But I won't be *that* cruel; only fair. So we'll go back to Ludwig and his *Mathematics*:

> The difficult thing here is not, to dig down to the ground; no, it is to recognize the ground that lies before us as ground.
>
> For the ground keeps giving us the illustory image of a greater depth, and when we seek to reach this, we keep on finding ourselves on the old level.
>
> Our disease is one of wanting to explain. [the 'why'. sg]
>
> [But] 'Once you have got hold of the rule [– as technique, application – sg], you have the route traced for you.'[6]

'Once you have got hold of the rule [as technique, application], you have the route traced for you.'

So, in looking more closely at this thing called sexual manners, the point of reference is precisely, for me, technique, application, i.e. the 'that of its existence. 'That they exist,' to echo Wittgenstein, 'is one of my foundations.'

Which is to say at least two things: First, that there is more than one foundation to 'truth' (and in this case sexual conduct is only one of many, a conduct which is, itself, multiple and discrete); and second, that foundations themselves can never be completely sealed, total, or homogeneous: can never be anything other than diverse; and in being diverse, never more than superficially so. For there is no greater depth to a ground (itself fractured and multiple): *only the surface*, only the superficial interplay of, in this case, the sexual game; only, that is to say, the play of the game. The game as play: the technique of artifice and pleasure and tension and passion and limit and pain and threshold and lust and juices and sport; all pulling on, all pulling on, all pulling with, all pulling against the Joke: the erasing and presencing of the truth, the erasing and presencing, simply, and to put it more accurately, of the game.

Which is to say two more things: that the Joke is neither real nor unreal; it is invention, whose meaning erupts through its style; contoured and shaped by its technique, always tossing and turning and erupting and demolishing within the play of the game. Indeed, with the Joke, we get into more serious matters: a side-stepping of confession, i.e., of having to 'confess' at every turn who it is we 'really' are, without losing the right to yell and kick and scream and be, well, be inconsistent. To be able to write over one's library door, as Vivian explained to Cyril, the word 'Whim'. For it is whim which suckles the teats of wisdom and creates in that suck the realm of the 'That': a fractured, quasi-mad Art form, an aesthetic of existence as Existence, an expression, a tension, a style, a play of the game which involves pleasure, and creativity, and fiction, and imagination and spectacle and beauty in all its sublime corrosiveness, false eyelashes, leather, and decay. In short, a 'that' which involves a certain kind of courage, I suppose, a courage to refuse the *Profound*, and exchange it, mixed metaphors and all, for the surface of the risk.

The Joke. The Joke is not 'on us': it *is* us. When it's worn as a badge of courage, it's called 'camp'. When it's flung against discriminating faults in reality, it's called 'irony'. When it's used to cement a collective identity as something more breathable, more changeable, more (happily) inconsistent than this thing named 'the community', it's called gossip. All at the surface of the risk. And we use our camp, our irony, our gossip as fleeting quantum, bubbling nodal points to invent *the story*, the story of our lives, a story with no *morals*, no *morals* to the story. We begin to re-create the queer 'we', accent on the comportment of oneself to the self; a funny, odd kind of collective enterprise, circumscribing and circumscribed by an impossible geography, existing and not existing in the context of our gossipy little narratives of the 'that' of our sexual habits, conducts, manners ... a 'that', I would venture to say, only able to exist in the 'elsewhere' of decadent urban life.

So, I put her in the cab. I was bored, annoyed. I wanted sex and I wanted it: tonight. I started wandering into the twilight of the city. I needed the walk. I needed to feel the air, damp and sweet, clinging against my body. As I turned the corner onto the Track site of the ghetto, there silhouetted against a wrought iron stairwell, were two beings. One had her skirt hiked up over her waist rocking violently above unthinkably high, high-heels; the other, on her knees, with one hand raised over the boundaries of the skirt, reaching upward toward the nipple, her other hand, the whole hand, lost somewhere deep inside the girl's cunt, pressing and pushing ... And I stood there, staring. Staring at the sight of their bodies so utterly connected; taking in the sounds of their moans, the pungent smells of their sweat: forbidden and intoxicating all at once. Drinking in the scene, spellbound as I was from watching the nails of the one tear convulsively into the shoulders of the other. A feast so lushly displayed in front of me ... it did not matter which one beckoned to me first.

Nor did it matter that, in the end, I never found out their names.

Sexual manners: an effrontery to morals, a conduct taken not 'despite all odds' but *in the face of them*, laughing in the face of them. Understanding the Joke: in 'I am Curious, Yellow'.

And we are curious, pink.

Notes

[1] 'Sexual Manners' was first presented in Toronto and sponsored by Public Access, April 15, 1992, and appears in *Public*, Summer 1993.
[2] Ludwig Wittgenstein, *On Certainty*, edited by G.E.M. Anscombe and G.H. von Wright; translated by Denis Paul and G.E.M. Anscombe, (Oxford: Basil Blackwell, 1974), pp. 18e-19e.
[3] Ludwig Wittgenstein, *Remarks on the Foundations of Mathematics (Revised Edition)*, edited by G.H. von Wright, R. Rhees, G.E.M. Anscombe. (Cambridge/London: MIT Press, 1983), Part VII, p355 (#1).
[4] *Ibid*, Part VI, p350 (#46).
[5] *Ibid*, Part VI, p303 (#2).
[6] *Ibid*, Part VI, p333 (#31).

Dynamics of Desire

DELLA GRACE

> Images exist; things themselves are images … Images constantly act on and react to one another, produce and consume. There is no difference between images, things and movement …'[1]

As a photographer who deals in seduction and exchange I have been wondering why it is that people allow themselves to be photographed by me in what you could call compromising positions. Although I usually pay travel expenses, give them prints and occasionally a bit of money, if I am being paid, the incentive to 'pose, perform or model' for me isn't financial. I ask them to submit to my fantasies and to confess their own to me. At times they may be in great physical discomfort and occasionally at risk, from the law or the less than law abiding, who wish to censor their display. Is it any more than narcissistic pleasure? Or an overwhelming 'desire to speak sex and hear it spoken?'[2]

In this piece I want to examine what I call the 'photographic moments' in terms of some of the processes involved. Those seldom seen and rarely talked about moments that exist before the image is created and after the image is 'consumed' by the spectator. Traditionally the relationship between the photographer and model is gendered, with the male being the photographer and the female being the photographer's object. What might an image look like if both the photographer and the photographed inhabited the subject position, or even if the subject-object dynamics oscillated between them in a way that caused the spectator to question his or her own positioning? It is this 'play of looks' that I want to explore, within the framework of desire and its visual representations. By unearthing some of the psychical, social and sexual processes involved in

90

representations of desire we can begin hopefully to examine the dynamics of desire present in the relationship between the photographer, the photographed and you.

I find the people I want to photograph everywhere. They are the people about whom I find something irresistible. I may be walking down the street, or on a bus, in a club or a café when I see *her*.[3] She has caught my eye. I look. Giving myself permission to look. I may even find myself staring, lost in the fantasy of her face. She has a presence that captures me completely. I want her. I want to see. I want to know. I want to have, if only for an instant. This is my most vulnerable moment. If my gaze is returned I try to smile and not let the embarrassment at being caught looking, caught with my desire exposed for all to see, jeopardize what could be the start of something wonderful. If I am feeling particularly dashing I will walk over and introduce myself by way of my fascination with her face and form. I will briefly state my purpose and if she is responsive to this, suggest we meet at a later date to discuss my proposition in greater detail. If this initial seduction is successful, (which it usually is when I feel dashing), we move on to the negotiation stage. This can either be a continuation of the seduction or simply a stating of boundaries, hopes and fears that eventually leads to the photographic moment. Not the 'Decisive Moment' so treasured by Cartier-Bresson, but a series of moments, from the instant my eye lands upon her body to the moment yours does.

In the beginning of my photographic career I worked under the assumption that the women I photographed agreed to do so from a position of defiance towards a feminist agenda that refused to include them as sex-positive perverts and dykes. In 'Dykography', Jan Zita Grover's essay on lesbian photographic representation, she states: 'In the case of the much commented upon anti-sexuality of much politically active lesbian writing and photography in the 1970s, one can see the downplaying of sexuality as a gesture of accommodation toward the heterosexual world of dominant culture, not only as a correction (reaction) to the prevailing male construction of the lesbian as perversely and exclusively sexual, but also as the price of being able to work alongside otherwise discomforted straight women.' She goes on to say, 'I think that much of our current self-representation has been effected at the expense of our sexuality, or at any rate of its representation. In seeking to represent the female sexual outlaw, the dyke, as a whole person, many photographers have ceased imagining her as a *hole* person.'[4] By the very act of allowing ourselves to be imaged as actively sexual and engaged in a variety of diverse and perverse practices we reclaimed the right to exist as we desire.

The technique I employed when photographing people in those early days had much to do with a lack of confidence and fear of being considered 'male identified'. The camera was thought of as an invasive and patriarchal (phallic) tool, the contemporary equivalent of the evil eye. Films such as Peeping Tom,[5] encapsulated the sadistic male gaze in the popular imagination. As a woman and a feminist I was loath to be associated with this approach.

For about the first ten years I took photographs, my style was influenced by fear. Fear of getting it wrong and so betraying my 'sisters'. Fear of being seen to enjoy power which was impure, a masculine imperative. I was reluctant to actually direct and create, rather than simply record images. I seldom took candid shots, not wanting to be seen as intrusive or exploitative. In a more formal, posed situation I would simply ask my models to 'be themselves' providing very little direction, or so I thought.

I now equate this approach with a lack of responsibility, a way of disowning the power of the relationship between the photographer and the photographed. I wanted to believe that I was simply a vehicle for my models' self-expression. Considering myself a 'pure channel' for the truthful representation of lesbian and gay culture was a way of exonerating and distancing myself from photography's voyeuristic and sadistic excesses.

When I negotiate a shoot today it is important that we are both conscious of what it means to create an image. The models must be aware that the image will travel, possibly in unanticipated ways. They need to be willing to sign a model release form that gives me permission to use the image at my discretion. Asking for this was not comfortable in the beginning, as it took our relationship out of the private/personal space we created for ourselves and brought it into a public/professional space that could seem to negate the model's power. However in order for both of us to feel safe a model release is essential, it becomes a kind of photographic condom.

When negotiating boundaries what I am actually asking for is unconditional consent. This consent is based on respect, trust, and a belief in the validity of our existence as well as the importance of making it visible. When I photograph dykes conversant with the etiquette of contemporary lesbian sadomasochism, the concept of unconditional consent is instantly understood. We know the rules because we made them up. I just need to know that we *are* speaking the same language. From me they need to know I have absolute respect for who they are and total admiration for the courage it requires to surrender themselves.

During the shoot I invite them to submit to my vision, to put themselves and their latent image in my capable hands. Our roles are clearly defined. I want to see them and they want to see themselves being seen. They want to please me and my pleasure is inextricably bound up in theirs. I am allowed to be powerful, controlling and creative within the context of the photographic moment. The models allow themselves 'Permission to Play'[6] and to become something other than the selves they know. If my camera lens is phallic it is certainly not male, it is a lesbian cock, welcomed, even required. For if pleasure and knowledge are the quest then an active and penetrating vision must be allowed entry. 'Vision is not only a passive, feminine receptacle where the real gets photographed, but it is also a phalloid organ able to unfold and erect itself out of its cavity and point towards the visible. The gaze is the erection of the eye.'[7]

My desire is complex. I want the people I photograph in an extremely specific way and although this wanting is undeniably sexual, it is far from genital. If I said that a photo shoot is my way of *having* them without doing it, what would you understand by that? If I said that the high I get during a successful photo session is more satisfying than multiple orgasms or even my favourite foods, would you understand my definition of *having*? Although there is an element of possession involved, (in law I own the image) *having* is not possessing. Possession is a kind of permanent having that implies power over someone or something. Having is a temporary condition of being, as in *having* (rather than possessing), an orgasm. In this context it is something both the photographer and the photographed can experience, though not necessarily simultaneously. During these moments the model *has* an absolute hold on my attention. I want them, I need them, I exist only to have them. We are irretrievably and symbiotically linked. This *is* a power relationship but neither of us have power *over* the other, rather, the power we have is fluidity itself. The images we create together give us a visual voice in a world that prefers our silence.

In a photo session shot for *Quim* magazine[8] I asked Skeeter and Aphra to enact a lesbian version of the Daddy/Boy scene.[9] Skeeter is a lesbian who identifies as a Daddy while her female lover becomes the Boy. 'Daddy Boy Dykes' is an exploration of the paradoxical role the Lesbian Cock plays in contemporary lesbian sexual practice. In this series you see what appear to be two gay men cruising each other. Next there are images of oral submission and anal pleasure. It is not until the final shot that biological gender of the two models is revealed. This last shot has the Boy looking with one eye at the viewer, her arm placed protectively around the shoulder of her Daddy, while the other hand holds her Daddy's cock possessively. The Daddy also holds her own cock as she looks at her Boy through dark glasses. In a feature for Skin Two's *Women With Attitude* about my work, Skeeter states: 'One of the reasons I feel comfortable working with Della is because although she has a set idea of what she wants, she allows you to interpret that and she wouldn't want you to compromise yourself and for there to be an image that you didn't feel comfortable with. So every photograph she's taken of me is how I want to be seen and I'm usually happy with the results because its nothing I wouldn't actually wear or do.'[10]

While it is true that I have an idea of what I'm after in a session, it is equally true that the images only come into focus through the process of our interaction. Every scenario is different and every model presents a new challenge. The process is truly symbiotic because their interpretation of my instructions can change the way I see and what I want. The more they allow me to create and be the *source* of this experience, the more confident I become, which in turn creates stronger images. As I take control of their bodies they are freed from the responsibility of having to construct their own image, allowing previously unknown aspects of themselves to emerge. This is part of the excitement, the thrill of the unknown, the suspense. The opportunity to see themselves through another's eyes, in the first instance, the actual photographic shoot, and in the second, to see themselves being seen by a multitude of eyes, when the photographs are exhibited and/or published. The key to the models' power lies precisely in her ability to surrender herself to the unknown. She is confident about her image travelling to unknown quarters and perhaps has a fantasy that as her image travels so does she. As others watch her, perhaps she is watching them …? There is a sense in which the model has triumphed over the evil eye by possessing it.

The pleasure and desire I experience is, of course, filled with trepidation and pain, for the moment I desire, I must face possible rejection, the possibility of technical failures, and the ultimate anxiety of having the work seen, and consequently judged, most likely *not* on my own terms. As the models are required to surrender themselves so must I, surrender and acknowledge that I have absolutely no control over how the images will be seen or interpreted. I have gone from the bottom to the top and back again. Desire being itself is never relinquished or achieved.

Notes

[1] Gilles Deleuze, 'Afterimage' no. 7, Summer 1978.

[2] Michel Foucault, *The History of Sexuality*, Volume 1, An Introduction, p51-73, Penguin, Harmondsworth, 1990.

[3] In this piece I will be using the feminine pronoun, assuming that the male reader will know to read himself into the scene.

[4] Jan Zita Grover, 'Dykography, Dykes in Context: Some Problems in Minority Representation', in *The Contest of Meaning*, ed R. Bolton, MIT Press, Cambridge, MA, 1992.

[5] Michael Powell, *Peeping Tom*, 1960, 35mm colour, 103 min.

[6] 'Permission to Play' was the motto of *Chain Reaction*, a lesbian s&m fetish niteclub, active between 1986-1990.

[7] Jean Clair, *La Pointe a l'oeil* (Paris: Cahier du Musée National d'Art Moderne, 1983) '*The visible that is pointed to is a new kind of visible, permitted only because of the space which has been created by the gaze of the pervert.*'

[8] *Quim*, Issue No. 3, 1991.

[9] The Daddy/Boy phenomenon is an offshoot of the gay, male, leather scene that an increasing number of lesbians are appropriating for themselves.

[10] Skin Two Video No. 4 – *Women With Attitude*, 1992.

I'd like to thank Parveen Adams, Lulu Bellreux, Philip Derbyshire, Sylvia MacFarland and Cherry Smyth for their encouragement and comments.

Lesbian Boys and Other Inverts

DELLA GRACE

Dyke Pussy Patrol # 1

Dyke Pussy Patrol # 2

Pleasure Principles

Dyke Pussy Patrol # 3

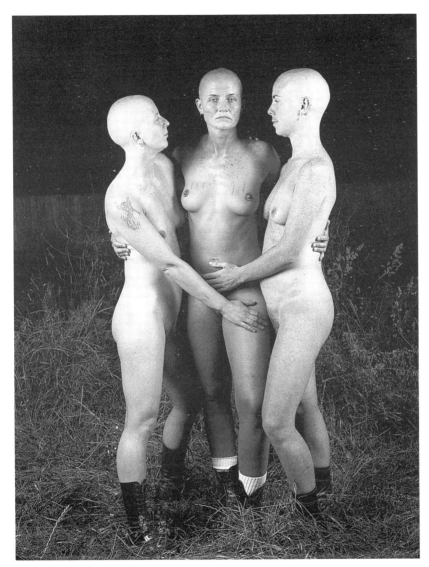

The Three Graces

Cyclops

Persephone

Intimate Inverts

Lola Flash

Queer x 3

The Gate Keeper

Lesbian Cock

Gay's the Word – Or Is It?

KENNETH MACKINNON

The Language of Dissent

The title of this article places emphasis on the language of dissent, treating this as worthy of serious consideration. The use of 'gay' as a positive or neutral term calculated to challenge the negative, medically pathologised connotations of 'homosexual' generates problems which vitally impinge on the crucial processes of self-identification and self-perception.

The term 'homosexual' refers to a sexuality; a sexuality which has been taken to explain an entire identity or personality type. The term 'gay', on the other hand, pushes the question of sexuality onto a new focus upon 'sensibility'. This shift marks both a critique of the medical category of homosexuality and a new focus on the politics of identity.

However, although the use of the term 'gay', and its focus upon 'sensibility', foregrounds the importance of language and the process of labelling as a question of politics, it does nothing to dismantle what could be argued to be the very source of the particular form of oppression known as homophobia; namely that certain persons are deemed separate and 'Other'. It maintains the distinctiveness and separateness of an identity which is defined fundamentally by its sexuality. Within this discourse of 'gayness' identities are reducible to and explicable by their sexuality. In fact, it could even be argued to reinforce the oppression by attaching new, adversative values to an old opposition without questioning the opposition itself. The opposition remains; only the values are inverted. 'Gay is good' – and 'Other'.

The Place of the Personal

In the field of sexual politics the personal has become a safe piece of ground. 'The personal is political' is a lesson gratefully learned from feminism. Nevertheless, it is a lesson that should not be taken at face value. Personal experience has so often been used as a basis for legitimising 'appropriate' sexual conduct. It is often conceived as the basis of a *truth* not only for oneself, but also for others.

The intention is not, however, to unmask the personal as if detecting its presence would of itself unseat the argument which makes appeal to it. The personal is at the very heart of what sense we can make of sexuality, or of sexuality as the imagined key to personal identity, in so far as these elements, sexuality and identity, have been mediated by authority, self-appointed or otherwise, without our society. Yet, the personal is not sufficient. Its meaning is certainly not self-evident.

Though aware of the risks of overtrusting the personal – paramountly the lurking possibility of failure to see the self as itself a construction – I would like to draw on some memories of my adolescence in the 50s and early 60s in the hope that these may yield some insights concerning society's present-day obsessions.

Sexual 'Knowledge'

In the 1950s, from the age of 11, I attended an academy – the equivalent of an English grammar school – in the Highlands of Scotland. This was a period often characterised as repressive or non-permissive.

In the second year at that school, girls were given sex talks, while boys were not. Some girls who felt no embarrassment at divulging the secrets of the talks informed us that they already knew more to begin with than the district nurse, equipped with slides of frogs, had told them. The boys concluded that it was rightly believed by the school authorities that male pupils 'knew it all already', and that that explained the decision not to discuss sex with them. So, boys and girls of no more than 13 years of age, were quite convinced that they already had adequate knowledge of sex without further instruction by the institution.

Several of them demonstrably did not have. My best friend and I had once looked within an illustrated medical book at the sketches of a pregnant woman's innards containing a liquid in which the fetus grew. Our conclusion was that the great secret of where babies came from involved a man's urination into a woman's belly. The idea held little charm for us, and seemed likely to hold little charm for the thus fertilised woman. When 'the facts of life' were finally explained by a boy who seemed to be sure of what he was talking about, they involved much slipping down and yanking up of gym shorts: the latter a precaution against the gym teacher's sudden unwelcome reappearance during furtive and speedy copulation. An element of play-acting and joking was evident even then in that explanation. There was much emphasis on physical skills. Most of these were concerned with evading discovery rather than with sexual 'technique'. We were well aware of an ever-watchful and censorious authority.

Behaviour

The boys talked about the girls and some seemed, even with the cool reappraisal of today's mature hindsight, to be mastering 'the facts of life', even outside the school gymnasium. Yet, it was noticeable – by tacit consensus rather than public declaration – that boys also experimented sexually with each other, as did, it seemed on evidence less available to me, the girls. While there was little mention of it, and certainly no public, straight-faced discussion of it, it happened. Everybody – at least all boys and presumably some girls – knew that it happened and apparently thought little about it. It seemed unremarkable that a boy who had been indulging in sexual games with one of his own sex should be seen the next evening on his first date with a girl pupil. None of us was surprised or commented with any seriousness on one boy's leap from one gender to another. Perhaps we saw ourselves in terms of Freud's polymorphous perversity rather than as end results of a successfully negotiated Oedipus complex.

Sexual 'Knowledge' and Hollywood Movies

By the age of 15, I was reading a number of sex manuals, borrowed from the town library, often in the light from the CinemaScope screen at one of the local cinemas. Today, it seems no accident that sex and the movies seemed inextricable from each other, or, in this case, that the search for sexual information and the loss of self-awareness when the screening absorbed my attention could so easily happen in the same location. The figure of the censorious gym teacher haunted the imaginings of my instructor in 'the facts of life'. The cinema, however, held one particular attraction: that it seemed to evade censorship, both in how it worked on spectators, and in what could be done – and read – in the darkness of the auditorium or the brilliance of light reflected from the wide screen.

At an obvious level, this judgment about late-'fifties cinema is patently ridiculous. How could Hollywood movies be thought to evade censorship, when the Production Code was still in force, driving the studios to self-censor in their best economic interests, when Hollywood was barely recovering from the McCarthy investigations (in which homosexuality was thought of as yet another manifestation of godless Communism and of anti-American alien infection)?

If the movies of the time had scenarios which were minutely inspected and rigorously vetted for impropriety and signs of anti-Americanism, however defined, we are only beginning during the last two decades to understand how the 'magic' of Hollywood may have worked. While Laura Mulvey has awakened us to awareness that Hollywood's regimes of looking may work to keep woman in her appointed place of submissiveness and passivity, she also recognises problems in the experience of the female spectator. If she 'enjoys' movies, is she 'masculinised'? Or is she temporarily transvestite?[1]

Freud might argue unregenerately that the female spectator receives masochistic pleasure in beholding her passivity. More interestingly, his work on fantasy suggests that the subject's relation to fantasy is constantly shifting and that we cannot predict from knowledge of the subject's gender, class or social positioning, for example, what sites of identification he or she will occupy in relation

112

to the scenario of fantasy.

In this way, movies' strong inbuilt patterns of psychological identification could still be thought to invite, for example, trans-gender dreaming, to offer experiences which did not simply heighten the existing experiences of differential power relations but which could allow these to be reordered to provide pleasures unavailable within quotidian experience. Whatever was going on 'in fact' in adolescents' personal lives, could be made sense of through fantasies which seemed quite remote from education and 'knowledge'. The sense might not survive into the daylight, but it is unlikely that it was discarded. Rather, there might be compartmen-talization or even ghettoization of experience, whereby there was an 'official' reality and patterns of sexual conduct side by side with a powerful, but unvoiced, alternative set of possibilities.

The Sex Manuals: the 'Homosexual Phase' and 'Normal Heterosexuality'

The manuals devoured in the secrecy of cinema front stalls provided an authority voice on sexuality, which was not quite the same voice as that of the district nurse heard by the girls, since, for one thing, it was listened to in a venue which seemed to exclude the school.

Nearly all the manuals assured the reader that there was a 'homosexual phase' during adolescence, that it was completely normal and unworrying, and that 'healthy' adolescents, male and female, came through this phase to 'normal heterosexuality'. Thus, it could be concluded, the experiementation between boys was downright normal too. Without it, the manuals seemed to affirm, there could not be the completion of the adolescent's natural and predestined sexuality.

The Birth of Homophobia

By the age of 17, armed with the reassurance of the manuals and fed by a generalised mythology about the 'otherness' and predatoriness of the homosexual (an invariably adult and devious character of ravening appetites), I had my first experience of violent homophobia. One of the most unimpeachably 'straight'-seeming

113

boys, who had a regular girlfriend and who was universally admired for his sporting achievements and his head-boy good looks made a serious attempt at my seduction. My phobic reaction was what the Greek root stresses – it was based on terror. It was a physical reaction involving nausea and, after the repulse of the attempt, a sleepless, anxious night.

The anxieties were indistinguishable from the bewilderment that I felt. How could somebody so 'straight' be so 'bent'? How could he have gone right through The Phase, gone out with his girlfriend (he later married her and she bore him children) like any other late-adolescent boy, and have such attractions still? Was I 'to blame', causing the deviancy in one within whom it surely did not belong?

Some Lessons

There are several lessons to be learned from these reminiscences.

One is that the notion that schoolkids are sexualised only by being exposed to sexual instruction is almost certainly idiotic. It would seem that adolescents will experience sex in one form or another, with or without making sense of it, whether or not it is 'explained', whether or not they are guided through it. What is also clear is that the version of sexual instruction which reaches them may set up problems for them. The love which nearly all my friends of that period had for Hollywood movies and for the stars of the 'fifties would suggest that the ignoring of fantasy and its multifariousness is perilous for educationists and moralists, whether concerned with instruction of the young or with attacks on the masturbatory pleasures of pornography.

Another is that homophobia may well have its roots in guilty attraction to the forbidden. (Another friend dreaded dates with girls to whom he was strongly attracted because he would become, quite literally, sick to his stomach when he kissed them. Life was a Woody Allen comedy of pain and humiliation to him. Suddenly he would have to terminate evenings out, at the point where the strength of his desire made him throw up.) Not everybody who claims that a particular form of sexuality makes him or her sick is lying or exaggerating. Extreme physical reactions need not be understood entirely in terms of moral outrage, however.

The preceding are lessons not likely to be required by the readers of this collection of essays. What may be more illuminating is my misperception of what seemed like a foolproof heterosexual and my troubled night when I was confronted with what was hitherto unthinkable, that somebody could move between a serious, and willingly chosen, commitment to a person of one gender to an attraction to one of his own gender.

The Threat of 'Bisexuality'

The term bisexuality has political mileage, at least in its conventional use, in that it appears to provide an explanation for individual refusal of, or inability to stay forever within, the parameters of two mutually exclusive sexualities. No defence is offered within this essay for retention of the category. In many ways it is inextricably linked to those two categories (homosexuality and heterosexuality) which it appears to traverse. Bisexuality is still seen as a crossing between two distinct and fixed sexualities. It might make more sense to cease basing categorisations of sexuality on object-choice and to return to what Freud refers to when he talks about 'polymorphous perversity'. However, a crucial part of this essay's aim is to examine the way in which sexuality is talked about and conceived, rather than to move into utopian territory with an imagined dismantling of conventional categories.

As I have said, the invention of bisexuality shores up the traditional explanations of sexuality. Nevertheless, the breaching of the borders surrounding sexualities – the conduct of bisexual acts and the crossing of points of sexual identification – could upset conventional sexual politics. Despite an element of chic about bisexuality, at least among stars in the middle seventies, the so-called bisexual is more commonly viewed as a traitor, or a fence-sitter, as being 'really' one thing or the other but too cowardly to 'come out' as one or the other.

Those who self-identify as heterosexual see the bisexual as sly and destructive. An added edge is given to the vituperation with the advent of AIDS, since the bisexual male, at least, can be saddled with the guilt for bringing HIV back to heterosexuals. In the mythology of AIDS, the male bisexual performs a vital function, in

115

that he is taken to confirm the 'natural' place of infection, and simultaneously to relieve the heterosexual of guilt for its presence in him or her.

For the self-identifying homosexual, the bisexual, male or female, is conceived as a half-closeted figure, not sufficiently 'out' to bear responsibility, yet not sufficiently convincing in dedication to heterosexuality to be taken as anything but 'really gay'.

The terms within which sexual politics can normally expect to be discussed involve the polarities of heterosexual and homosexual. The individual whose sexuality is not definable within these polarities is taken to be an almost imponderable entity which has failed, so far, to have the courage of his/her convictions. Thus, even that figure which most undermines the belief in the possibility of exclusive categories is colonised by one side or the other in this antithesis, saddled with a range of unattractive personal qualities which are thought to explain that individual's 'indecision'.

It is particularly dismaying to find this thought process going on in persons who have themselves been deemed to be, by nature, 'neurotic' or 'oversensitive' and who have had these attributions explained by their sexuality. Those who would comfortably hold on to this account of the 'essentially' homosexual attributes of hypersensitivity or emotional 'instability' seem not to give any weight to the fact that this particular sexuality is stigmatised in a homophobic society. The 'bisexual' has often been judged as shallow and treacherous by nature. There is an alternative, though; that 'bisexuality' is not allowed to fit within the dominant picture of sexuality, so that the 'bisexual' must shift allegiances to belong at all, even temporarily. Both of these explanations may be too pat, but the second is at least worth considering as an option.

If, more germanely and directly, we see sexuality as a continuum, instead of as a matter of binary oppositions, the picture alters dramatically. Morever, it is a picture where certain shadowy figures, certain obscure areas, may emerge in a clearer light.

The analogy of the continuum has its drawbacks, all the same. Once again, although attention may be focused on the middle areas, it can be a continuum only by virtue of the fixed points, the extremes at either end. By this means, the separate and dramatically differentiated sexualities, hetero- and homo-, stage a grand re-entry just when they seemed discardable. The grey area can be identified as such only because the white and black at each end of the continuum are so clearly discernible. Rather than scrabbling around for a less assailable metaphor, we may have to recognise that there cannot be new thinking on sexuality until the categories are demolished. Each analogy tends to reify them. Attention may be more usefully directed towards a sceptical reinvestigation of the current picture and what we are asked to credit to maintain that picture.

The Phase Re-Examined: The Difficulty of Sustaining Separation

What is the sense of a phase which prepares adolescents for heterosexuality precisely by immersing them in what is culturally taken to be its polar opposite? If the question becomes meaningless because it implies a quasi- or truly divine providence in human development, why, quite simply, should there be a homosexual phase at all, unless recourse is had, within the discourse of the natural, to further notions, of health and disease? If so, this *phase* of adolescent homosexuality could be explained as a kind of inoculation against disease by early exposure to it (heterosexuality developing under the benign influence of psychic antigens). But why doesn't the inoculation always 'take?' Why the prohibitions against the disease, if the *phase* has a quasi-medical explanation of this sort? Why has the inoculation such partial and unimpressive effects? Why is the disease so attractive that societal policing of heterosexual boundaries is necessitated?

Freud's version of sexual development, for example, raises a further question by explaining the passage from polymorphous perversity into heterosexuality as involving the suppression of homosexuality; why is homosexuality not explained by him as involving the suppression of heterosexuality? If that conclusion is implicit in Freud, why has he not made it explicit?

A host of other questions suggest themselves. By what criteria, for example, can porn stars who have committed numerous acts of fellatio and anal intercourse, both active and passive, with other men, state in interviews, and expect to be taken seriously, that they are 'really' heterosexual? Can notions of good acting cover this emergency?

Or, for example, with what cogency can homosexual activity within prison be explained away as a temporary aberration from the norm of natural heterosexuality? These activities are often sanctioned within a culture of rampant homophobia which perhaps relates to the way in which sex is manifested in that setting.

Dealing with Categorisation

The categories of the homosexual and heterosexual cannot be dissolved by an act of will. Many are now aware that the homosexual (person) was invented by medical opinion in the last century. Where there were acts which could with greater ease be labelled heterosexual and homosexual, suddenly at that point there were people who with far more difficulty were labelled heterosexual or homosexual. If the latter label was applied, then the entire being of the person might, it seems, be explained by appeal to the label as if it encapsulated the totality and potentiality of the person thus labelled.

Labelling had, and continues to have, disastrous consequences. The most obvious sense of this statement is that those with the 'wrong' label may face imprisonment, torture, death, and at the very least humiliation and social ostracism. Those bearing the wrong label found themselves in death camps in Nazi Germany. Those fighting for equal housing rights in the late 1970s, in Dade Country, Florida, found themselves democratically defeated by Anita Bryant – with God on her side.[2]

The sufferings of certain persons with AIDS would seem to be just recompence for 'unacceptable' lifestyles, if they happen to be wearing the wrong label. David Blunkett of the Labour Party felt free to talk about Freddie Mercury's alleged 'bizarre lifestyle' in BBC1's *Question Time* of 28th November 1991, the day after Mercury's funeral, as if this lifestyle in some way denied him the right to sympathy for his death.

Even more importantly, the frequent suggestions within mass media that HIV attacks homosexuals and not normally heterosexuals makes the gross error, apart from its ignoring of evidence from

Africa, of investing a virus with a personality and a moralism which would have it seeking out one category of person and by-passing another, like the Angel of Death in ancient Egypt. Everything that we think we know about HIV suggests that certain *practices* render persons vulnerable to the virus and that certain other practices, included among which is, importantly, 'safe sex', renders the same persons far less vulnerable. The way that information about AIDS has been created and relayed by a media anxious to perpetuate the dichotomy of persons on the basis of sexuality would suggest that the belief in the dichotomy can quite literally mean the difference between life and death.

Heterosexuality is seldom seen as problematic enough to require defending or explicating, since it has as a constant alibi the imagined virtues of reproduction. Where controversy does arise in the sphere of heterosexuality, it is usually over the Pill, or abortion, since these suggests that heterosexuality may be enjoyed by some for its own sake and not in the cause of reproduction.

God and the Discourse of Nature

By far the most important observation, though, is that the most reactionary, fundamentalist accounts of the God-given and 'natural' quality of heterosexuality betray an unadmitted (because totally suppressed?) inability to believe their own claims.

If heterosexuality is so natural, why has there to be such dedicated protection of the impressionable from even hearing about an alternative? If no less a being than God protects the heterosexual from the satanic alternative, why does there have to be such vigorous intervention by the state in this country to ensure that homosexuality and 'pretended family relationships' are not 'promoted', when everywhere in popular media heterosexuality is indeed advertised and promoted?

It is at least curious that in Britain in the vaunted age of enterprise there was such panic in the late 'eighties that there had to be massive state intervention in, as it were, the free market in sexuality, that restrictive practices had to be introduced, protectionism allowed, all in the name of keeping heterosexuality flourishing. When the Thatcher government pretended to be impressed by feminist arguments about pornography and the harm it caused to women, it is curious that the result of this vaunted openness to feminist argument is that porn designed for homosexual spectators appears to have had a tougher time of it than that promoting a peculiarly explicit version of heterosexuality.

One conclusion could be that right-wing spokespersons on behalf of heterosexuality, of 'nature' and God's will, are hypocritical bigots, dressing up their intolerance and prejudice in the clothes of religiosity and pseudo-biology.

The credibility of an attribution of sexual obsession to the moral conservatives seems to be indicated by their claimed reliance on the word of God, as revealed in the Bible, to render its 'natural' repugnance as obedience to divine teachings. Yet, there is no commandment against homosexuality. There is one against covetousness. Christ seems to have been far more clearly and explicitly repelled by the rich man than by homosexuality. The same devout fundamentalists who search the Scriptures for signs that they have God as their ally when they preach hellfire and damnation for 'gay militants' seem to be quite untroubled by the expressions of disapproval for the acquisitive.

An altogether more interesting conclusion would be that reactionary thinkers are alarmed by their own ill-suppressed 'knowledge', their awareness that the dividing lines between the sexualities are not nearly as clear as they would like them to be, that the myth of the exclusive, 'natural' heterosexual has to be shored up against the weight of evidence against its credibility, that they must insist on its truth at the very point when they become most acutely aware of its unlikelihood.

'Liberationist' Retention of the Categories

Given the history of brutal oppression of those labelled homosexual, it is fully understandable that political movements dedicated to the redressing of such evils should reassess the meaning of the label, should substitute gay pride for homosexual self-hatred, should concentrate on the achievements of 'gays' so identified, throughout human history. One obvious problem in this approach is that it seems to valorise the category of the heterosexual even as it accepts and perpetuates in new, improved form the category of the homosexual.

Such categorisation, involving heterosexual/homosexual and gay/straight, inevitably helps to produce 'reality'. If individuals are socialised through their upbringing in cultures which habitually separate sexualities, which habitually promote one form of sexuality and stigmatise another, then they will internalise to a profound extent the dichotomy and the social attitudes. In so doing, they make the dichotomy 'real' even if at one point in history it might not have been so. Given that men and women are encouraged to see themselves as one personality type or the other, and are provided with no viable alternative, it is not surprising that millions see themselves as that type and not the other. We have an extraordinary situation, where types seem to have been made 'real' and yet may not ultimately be true. The evidence of their falsity keeps leaking out, but because official ideology and counter-tactics to it cannot allow themselves to deal with the evidence, this evidence is viewed as unreadable and thus in some way discarded.

Categorisation and Sexualities – the Future

One alternative has been to invest 'the homosexual' with a 'sensibility', which is usually termed 'gay'. At a stroke, however, the move further reifies the homosexual person, separates him or her from other persons outside 'gayness' by means of special attributes, and obfuscates the basic problem of the intolerance shown to a particular sexuality by shifting attention from the homosexual to the full-rounded gay person.

Of what does this gay sensibility (male version) consist, though? It has variously been identified with camp, with disco, with Judy Garland, with playfulness (particularly around societal fixity of the masculine and feminine). What, then, of the homosexual male who cannot appreciate camp, who does not like Garland or disco, who is not playful? Is this person not blessed with a gay sensibility? Does he, then, not deserve the rights that are usually identified as 'Gay Rights'?

The increasing desperation of the search for the separable gay sensibility became striking in two issues touched upon in Channel

121

4's *Out* series (which takes as its brief the exploration of lesbian and gay experience and issues). The questions which were addressed were, Is the treatment of domestic pets as surrogate children an exclusively gay phenomenon? and Is there really such a thing as 'gay food'? (Perhaps the second being 'playfully' proposed? Does that make the proposition, but not the food, 'gay'?)

The predominant message from gay activists today suggests that homosexuals are different but (at least) equally valuable within society. The eagerness with which American Gay rights groups seized on 'scientific proof' that gay men's brains were formed like women's suggests an alarming interest in going for biology, abandoning the complexity of arguments related to the concept of 'chosen sexuality' in the face of those who would argue simplistically that (any) choice implies moral responsibility. This eagerness in turn implies that securing of grudging pity is preferable to dignified defiance of right-wing conservative thought on sexuality.

It seems to me important to refuse the self-evident nature of the label of 'the heterosexual'. Each time that category goes unchallenged, the separability of 'the homosexual', whereby that person may be objectified, dehumanised, eradicated, is permitted to go unchallenged. Likewise the word 'gay', and the conceptions of the homosexual person which the term helps to keep alive, may serve a less useful purpose than a sustained attack on the notion of the dichotomising and categorising of human beings through fetishistic insistence on their sexuality.

Notes and Further Reading

[1] Mulvey, Laura, *Visual and Other Pleasures*, London, Macmillan, 1989.

[2] Bryant, Anita, *The Anita Bryant Story*, Tappan, NJ, Fleming H. Reveil Company, 1977.

Crawford, Alan, *Thunder on the Right: The 'Bew Right' and the Politics of Resentment*, New York, Pantheon, 1980.

Foucault, Michel, *The History of Sexuality*, vol. 1, tr. Robert Hurley, Harmondsworth, Penguin, 1981.

Jorstad, Erling, *The Politics of Moralism: The New Christian Right in American Life*, Minneapolis, Augsburg Publishing House, 1981.

Mosse, George L., *Nationalism and Sexuality: Respectability and Abnormal Sexuality in Modern Europe*, New York, Howard Fertig, 1985.

Mount, Ferdinand, *The Subversive Family: An Alternative History of Love and Marriage*, London, Jonathan Cape, 1982.

National Deviancy Conference (ed.), *Permissiveness and Control: The fate of the sixties legislation*, London, Macmillan, 1980.

Plummer, Kenneth, *The Making of the Modern Homosexual*, London, Hutchinson, 1981.

Schur, Edwin M., *The Politics of Deviance: Stigma Contests and the Uses of Power*, Englewood Cliffs, NJ, Prentice-Hall, Inc., 1980.

Weeks, Jeffrey, *Coming Out: Homosexual Politics in Britain, from the Nineteenth Century to the Present*, London, Quartet Books, 1977, repr. 1983.

Weeks, Jeffrey, *Sex, Politics and Society: The regulation of sexuality since 1800*, London, Longman, 1981.

Weeks, Jeffrey, *Sexuality and its Discontents: Meanings, Myths and Modern Sexualities*, London, Routledge and Kegan Paul, 1985.

I should like to place on record the helpfulness and tact shown by David Oswell in his reading of this essay's first draft. The present version was much improved by his commentary on the original.

Performing Sexualities

INTERVIEW WITH ISAAC JULIEN

The following is an interview which took place in late 1992 in a Primrose Hill cafe between the film-maker Isaac Julien and David Oswell and Sean Nixon.

Men, Music, Clubs and Locality

Q. Dance, music, and style are important sites of sexual performance and masquerade. They play an important part in your film *Young Soul Rebels* (1991). Can you talk about their significance to you?

Isaac Julien (IJ): In the late seventies as a young black person I was into disco and soul music. I was also involved in socialist youth organisations, like the Workers' Revolutionary Party. Those sort of organisations, but also the left generally, were very puritanical and anti-pleasure. Many saw 'disco' as purely profit-motivated. My idea of going to clubs was very different from that being written about in certain left journals. For me there wasn't this tension between being a socialist and going to clubs.

The clubs provided an important cultural space. There were some people who would listen to soul music on the radio in their homes. But at that time there was very limited air space for soul or Black music in general. Some of us met in records shops to buy imported funk/jazz records. There was one really great record shop called *Contemp* just off the Tottenham Court Road. There was a huge audience who wanted to listen to that music and went to specialised record shops. And more and more of us converged around the clubs.

My experience of going to places like *Lacy Lady* and *Global*

Village (soul clubs in Ilford and Charing Cross) was that there were very few places where black people met *en masse*. We converged around reggae, disco music and soul. It was something we took great pleasure in. There was a sort of black Atlantic call and response dialectic at work in the reception of black American music and the way it was used and consumed in London clubs. It was the beginning of the formation of a new sort of public which wasn't being addressed anywhere else. You had this convergence of different audiences listening to disco and funk/jazz music. I felt there was this assemblage of different identities on the dance floor: black and white, middle class and working class, gay and straight. It was a hybrid space. It was the beginning of club culture as we know it now.

Richard Dyer was one of the few white intellectuals on the left to take disco seriously. I remember reading 'In defence of disco' (1979) in *Gay Left* magazine[1] and thinking 'Oh God, there's somebody on the level who doesn't think disco is decadent and anti-socialist'. He understood its pleasures and how it related to everyday life. Dick Hebdige had done the same sort of thing in *Subculture: the Meaning of Style* (1979)[2] with punk and reggae. I suppose, in many ways, *Young Soul Rebels* was a continuation of that dialogue.

When I went to some clubs it felt more liberatory than going to reggae clubs. If you were gay it was quite hard work going to a reggae club. In terms of gender and the forming of sexual identities, they were very strict. Whereas in those clubs which played disco there was more space given to playing with your identities and masquerade, although at the time it was still quite difficult. Those into reggae were very critical of soul and disco. There was a certain moralism. They thought I had sold-out. They thought I was more materialistic and more white-identified.

This was the beginning of club culture which really exploded in the late seventies and early eighties. It emerged from those underground movements which weren't political in any traditional sense. They were constituted around desires and fantasies. And at that moment, in the mid-seventies, this was completely overlooked.

In a sense, *Young Soul Rebels* is a slightly utopian and nostalgic, but necessary, vision of that formation. As I said, the film is, in many ways, an engagement with Hebdige's *Subculture*, I'm reclaiming and reconstructing an iconography of black British style from the seventies. There is, as it were, an 'official archive' of British subcultures on the left. At that time you were either into punk or, if you were black, into dread or afro. I wanted to rewrite the history and insert a more complex understanding of different black, sexual and gender identities.

Q. In that sense, what you're talking about is a complete reversal of traditional politics which says: first sort out the politics, then choose the lifestyle.

IJ: That's right. Mustn't have too many contradictions!

Q. Do you think that soul still provides that hybrid space in the nineties? Has the club scene got more segmented and less hybrid?

IJ: In the seventies choice was limited in terms of what places/spaces we could converge around. Some black soul boys tried to get into gay clubs because they played 'good' music. But this wasn't because they were gay. Of course not! [ironic laughter] It was one of the few places that you could listen to funk, etc.

That's very different from the eighties and nineties. Now there's a real pluralisation of places. There's a demarcation of types of spaces. Now people are, in a sense, more specific.

Q. Can I be provocative and suggest that this pleasure or desire for the hybrid – this concern with fragmented identities around race, gender and sexuality – is part of, at least in terms of what you've said about the club scene, a particular regime of taste, a specifically metropolitan set of preferences. Don't many people want a fixed sense of identity – especially, perhaps, sexual identity?

IJ: The thing is I want everybody to be like me [laughs]. I can understand why people want to be fixed, to have some certainty about who they are. But I think there are real problems with this kind of disavowing the contradictory structure of feelings, identifications and fantasies we all have.

I do feel that when I'm talking, I'm talking about the urban, I'm speaking from a certain place, I was born in the city. The films that I make are about those experiences in the city.

I wasn't born in the countryside, I don't like the countryside, especially the English countryside. I don't respect the values of Englishness which are embedded within that culture. I see myself contesting those values and those spaces, although I realise we have a right to claim it, if we want.

In film funding institutions people use the countryside (a certain type of regionalism and ethnicity) in order to suppress things which are going on in the city. In this sense I'm talking about the 'metropolitanness' of my identity as a form of celebration of the urban. I realise the limitations of that, namely the stereotyping of the black and the urban, but I do think that within those spaces there are a lot of things to celebrate. For example, the way in which blacks have transformed their position in the capital from the margins to the mainstream. I enjoy the way in which we have some cultural ownership of the city.

Likewise with suburbia. Suburbia, to put it crudely, has been that place where white people moved to get away from blacks. It has some hidden secrets. Some of the clubs I went to were in suburbia – like *Lacy Lady*. The only thing I find interesting about suburbia is the way in which David Lynch represents suburbia – this dark, cruel, interesting place. It's something I can't really take seriously – especially in relation to 'gay culture'. I know there's contestation about the 'metropolitanness' of queer cinema. But what would be my investment in appealing to suburbia or countryside places?

Q. I want to return, now, to some questions you raised earlier. I want to think a bit more about sexuality and gender and how that intersects with race and ethnicity. And I want to think about this in terms of questions of place. One of the things about your film, *Young Soul Rebels*, and also Stephen Frears' and Hanif Kureishi's *My Beautiful Laundrette*, (1985) is the intimacy in the way in which masculinity and sexuality are represented as being lived out within a particular locality which is cut across by the differences of race and ethnicity.

127

IJ: In the film I wanted to call attention to the play around black masculinity in the seventies, to the negotiation of those identities at an everyday level. There was much violence, but there was a certain performance and masquerade of different notions of masculinity in relation to ethnicity and race and also to locality. There was a shared knowledge and intimacy in relation to gender, sexuality, race and ethnicity. Black and white working class young people had grown-up together in the East End of London. So this racial trajectory was beginning to inform our identities – both black and white.

Obviously that intimate knowledge we had about one another is important. I think there is an ambivalent attraction and disavowal. The question of empathy/envy is very much a residue of the projection of white communities' desires and fears around 'black' sexuality. This is evident in relation to questions about black style. There is a way of walking, talking, standing and communicating in black 'masculine' culture. It was obviously something that the skinheads were envious of and trying to negotiate in their dress and music and so on (cf. Hebdige, 1979). But what I was trying to propose was that this type of racial negotiation around identities isn't always an 'Us' and 'Them' negotiation. It's about a sort of intimacy which is shared at the same time as it is disavowed, but in a very complicated way.

When I was growing up in the East End I remember seeing lots of black skinheads in the sixties. And that sort of died out with the construction of the 'white skinhead'. The film is very much about white envy as well as the assertion of young white and black gay lifestyles at that time. But then you had to choose whether you were an essential white subject or an essential black subject. But really when you look at the encounters, the conversations and dialogue of these groups of young people, you see a much more intimate knowledge of each other than is admitted. It's not as 'white' and 'black' as it might first appear. The left, then, often just looks at the simplistic opposition between white skinheads and blacks and Asians without understanding the complexity of the situation.

Film-making and Representational Strategies

Q. I want, now, to shift the focus onto your work as a film-maker.

Young Soul Rebels marks a shift from you earlier work with Sankofa or *Looking for Langston* (1989). You seem to be addressing a more popular audience. Does this mean a different way of negotiating sexual and racial politics?

IJ: I suppose the first thing to say is that I don't really see it as a shift, I think that there's a problem with the way that people talk about 'film'. Cultural critics seem to be entrapped in a division between high culture and popular culture.

I have a deep suspicion of this binary opposition. In the twenties and thirties black modernist painters were criticised by white patrons and critics because it wasn't what those critics considered as 'black art'. I have the same sort of problems thrown at me in relation to my film-making. There's a real resistance from both critics and institutions to black film-makers occupying an art cinema space. It's as if to properly engage politically you have to address 'the popular'. I'm interested in trying to break down those sort of divisions – like high culture/popular culture, art cinema/popular film. Obviously someone like Spike Lee does the same sort of thing. His films will be shown at a Cannon cinema and also at an art house cinema. This was the sort of release that *Young Soul Rebels* got in this country.

The question of economics comes in here too. Obviously *Young Soul Rebels* costs more. (Its budget was £1.25m). It would have been difficult in this country to get the same sort of money for *Looking for Langston*, an experimental film essay (whose budget was £100,000). This raises a number of questions about what kinds of films black film-makers, can, or are supposed to, make.

Everyone – both black and white cultural critics, commissioning editors and so on – wants you to solve this problem of 'the audience', in terms of representativeness, which I don't think is necessarily the film-maker's problem to solve.

One of the problems for film-makers like myself is that you want to resist categorisation. You actually want to make it difficult for people to categorise your work.

Q. I agree with you that there are problems with the politics of these oppositions, but, nevertheless, wouldn't you agree that these oppositions bear upon the way in which sexuality can be represented in films. For example, the figuring of sexuality in *Looking for Langston* is very different from what you do in *Young Soul Rebels*.

IJ: I think that they are different, but I don't think they're as different as people would like to make out. In *Young Soul Rebels* I don't adhere to the generic conventions of popular film. I give more attention to distantiation, to decor, to the range of shots, to the way that characters look at each other and to the way that the film was cut.

I think that *Looking for Langston* was a film which was probably seen by a predominantly white gay audience in the cinema. Whereas with *Young Soul Rebels* I felt that I was introducing all sorts of questions about sexuality and black queerness to a black audience because *Young Soul Rebels* was marketed as a 'black film'. In doing that I'm directly contesting what people value in the new black cinema. I'm contesting certain audience expectations. Those audiences want to see genre replications of *Boyz 'n the Hood* (1992). They want to see black masculinity represented in this hard sort of way. They don't want to see images of black and white gay men kissing on screen (or maybe some of them might). I think that there have been real problems with the recent celebration of black popular culture – which is about popular fantasies and myths of certain black homophobic masculinity in the cinema.

Against the desires and wishes of a lot of heterosexual black audiences, I want to push those questions about sexuality into that sort of cinematic space. Although, how successfully that is achieved I don't know. But I think politically it is important. It is part of my wider strategic cultural practice which comes very much from being involved in a London gay black group in the early eighties.

I think underlying those questions about how to address the audience are a set of moral questions. There is an argument which says that I, and other black and gay film-makers, should be constructing 'positive representations' to make people feel better in some sort of way when they go to the cinema. Cinema as a form of social work. I want to contest that, of course, and this is where 'Queer cinema' and 'Queer politics' becomes, for me, very interesting.

Q. Would you identify your filmic work within that wider category of 'Queer cinema'?

IJ: The thing I, strategically, enjoy about the recent labelling 'Queer' for my work is that it locates it not merely as gay or black film. I think a lot of the work of Black Audio Film Collective is very 'Queer'. It raises so many questions about cultural critique and how you address audiences. In other words when I think of 'Queer cinema', I think of it as having a much wider sense than films made by lesbian and gays. I think also, in some instances for me, it replaces the notion of 'Third cinema'.

'Queer cinema' contests the debate about 'positive' and 'negative' images. It contests the realism of that aesthetic/political strategy. It contests that conservatism. It suggests a more complex strategy for those audiences, such as blacks and gays, who have seen themselves as unrepresented in the dominant media culture.

I think that the question of essentialism is very important in terms of identity politics. Some people want a cinema made by authors who are black or gay/lesbian or both to make images which are for them. If you're politically on the left, you're aware of those questions about representation and identity. There is a policing of those images which are made by film-makers who are black or gay or both, because the burden of representation is heavily shouldered by us – sometimes in direct opposition to our identities as political artists and cultural activists.

Q. One of the problems that any cinema which deals with sexuality must face at some level is the problems of censorship. Has that been a problem for you?

IJ: A friend said to me the other day, 'You've never had full frontal nudity in your films', I said, 'No, this is true!' It's an impossible problem. Questions of sexuality are constantly being negotiated and renegotiated. Commissioning editors at Channel Four are always saying to me that I can't have erections in my films, so in my last film, *The Attendant* (1993), there are dildos. In relation to questions of censorship it was quite interesting. When I showed it to a black , gay, Dutch, film-maker friend of mine called Felix DeRoy, he said,

Pleasure Principles

'When I look at *The Attendant*, it's as if you are kicking this glass plate window. But you're caught in mid-action and your foot is just touching the surface'. Obviously living in Holland these questions of censorship are not such a big issue as they are in England. I thought this was an interesting way of describing what I'm doing and the way you are positioned in relation to censorship.

Both *Looking for Langston* and *Young Soul Rebels* have been censorship battles. *Young Soul Rebels* couldn't obtain a '15' certificate because of a sex scene. The British Board of Film Classification gave it an '18' because of the 'positive' affirmation of two men performing oral sex, smoking marijuana and drinking alcohol all at the same time. The only way it was going to get a '15' was if I cut the sex scene. This was a real problem because it meant that we couldn't advertise fully and get information across to those under 18, namely teenagers who are one of the prime target audiences. So in some way censorship constructs the type of audience that certain images can be shown to. In fact, I shot the film with this censorship in mind. That is why the love-making scene between Billybudd and Caz was shot in one take.

However, there is more censorship in television that there is in cinema. This is particularly problematic when these days the film industry is kept alive by television. Films have to be shown both in the cinema and on television.

Q. Again there is that policing of sexualities and a policing of hybridity. What is it about 'Queer cinema' that is different from earlier gay film making?

IJ: I don't really see this as a shift or a break. But before I talk about this, I think that it's important to use an example to point out the expediency at work in these debates. Whereas it took us 8 years to get the Institute of Contemporary Arts to stage a debate on black British independent cinema, it took them only 8 months to stage a conference on 'Queer cinema'.

It's interesting the way that 'Queer cinema' has emerged at the same time that aspects of gay culture, like camp, have been appropriated by heterosexuals – by David Lynch, for example, I think there's a strategic repositioning going on here.

I think that in Britain it's only seen as a fashion in the sense that some people are thinking in terms of: who's queerest? A sort of hierarchy of identities. In the States it comes out of a political movement of 'Queer' cultural activists. In this country it's been taken up as a fad, as a commodity. There's an interesting commodification going on here. This raises problems. For example, Madonna, in her book *Sex* plays around with images of blackness and gayness, S/M, and otherness.[3] She celebrates the erotic and the pornographic. I think that there are limits to transgressive acts. Madonna plays at being a dyke. She plays at being fucked by this black man. After a while it's like, so what! I think it's interesting the way that those images have been circulated in popular culture. The shift is important. But what are the political implications of this? I would want to put a question mark next to this.

I think that what's important is to make things more complex and contradictory. Placing ambivalence at the centre. Placing the margins at the centre. That's the place where I've been speaking from – from that hybrid space and I want my audiences to experience that too.

Q. This placing of the margins at the centre seems to be exactly what you do in your film *The Attendant*.

IJ: *The Attendant* was, in some ways, an aesthetic response to the 'Spanner Case'. [Editors: This was a case involving the prosecution and imprisonment of a group of gay men who had engaged in S/M practices]. It was commissioned by Channel Four for an art series to be shown throughout Europe. The film is concerned with fantasy and desire. It deals with questions about space and time. It's about memory and the representation of the black people who work in museums. The symbolic architecture of the museum forms the space in which the attendant has this S/M relationship – we don't know whether this is real or imagined.

There is no spoken dialogue. I constructed tableau vivants around a Biard painting 'Scene on the Coast of Africa', depicting slaves on a beach. This 18th century painting had a huge impact on me when I first saw it in a museum in Hull.

In the film, Stuart Hall looks at the painting. Hanif Kureishi and

Noman Rosenthal are visitors to the gallery. This forms a series of puns. The placing of a black cultural critic, a writer and a curator in these contexts. I have always been fascinated by the conjunction of plastic art and film and I wanted the film to interrupt certain assumptions about the relationship between black art and modernism. The black artist has always been seen by the modernist mainstream (the bastion of white, male, high culture) as a curiosity. Postmodernism, too, raises similar problems about the position of the black artist and the problem of representation.

Q. This brings us back to the question of hybridity.

IJ: I think that this hybridity in the field of vision of cinema is disturbing and makes people feel very uncomfortable. There is a certain amount of incommensurability between different identities. For example, I know that when some gay men went to see *Young Soul Rebels* in the cinema they had to deal with the violence and verbal homophobia of straight black audiences while watching the film.

Q. Do you feel that we need to rub up against that incommensurability?

IJ: I wanted to make audiences feel uncomfortable, to a certain extent, and challenge expectations especially those of the black straight audience. But I underestimated the reaction. It's not a comfortable experience and it worried me that gay men felt threatened.

Q. But aren't there different ways of rubbing up against difference. I mean that there are some situations where difference is just presented as conflict.

IJ: I think that cinema is one of the few domains where these differences can be negotiated especially as it takes place in the dark! [laughs] The role of fantasy should enable one to inhabit different subject positions and allow us to identify with characters, be they black or gay or both. But there is resistance.

Notes

[1] Richard Dyer, 'In defence of disco', *Gay Left* (1979) – reprinted in Simon Frith and Andrew Goodwin (eds.) *On Record*, Routledge, London, 1990.

[2] Dick Hebdige, *Subculture: the meaning of style*, Methuen, London, 1979.

[3] Madonna, *Sex*, Martin Secker and Warburg Ltd., London, 1992.

The Censor's Pleasure

GEOFFREY WOOD

What is it like to be a film and video censor? Pleasant though it might seem to be paid to watch films and videos, it does appear to be a somewhat dubious occupation, motivated, perhaps, by a very personal and morally repressive project, or maybe just the perfect pastime for a spoilsport? It is not inappropriate in talking about desire to talk about censorship. Indeed, it is necessary, but is it possible to discuss these in terms which are other than opposed? In the realm of desire can the role of the censor be anything other than simply to repress and is such repression purely negative? These are necessary questions for anyone who takes on such a seemingly damnable role and for a social-democratic politics.

I would like to address these questions, first to argue that censorship has to be taken seriously by those interested in cultural politics and to put a case for forms of regulation – a case which does not reply on a 'moral right' stance or a feminist anti-pornography position or a purely pragmatic approach. This will be brief, and extended arguments are to be found elsewhere,[1] but it is necessary for this account of the practice of censorship to be read other than with cynicism. Second, I would like to explain the way film and video censorship operates in this country and to give examples of the way in which policy works.

The Argument for Regulation

Censoriousness is usually associated with the political right from its clear moral positions centred on the nuclear family and its paternalistic heritage, though this has been muddied since the arrival of Thatcherism with its extreme free market viewpoints. The classic liberal tradition is centred on the freedom of the individual although it does give space for state restriction. This is underpinned theoretically by John Stuart Mill and the 'harm criterion'; the individual should be free to do what he or she wants unless these wants can be shown to harm others. The left has had a peculiar blindness to the idea of censorship, usually regarding it with anathema and identifying it with oppressive regimes such as Stalinism or Nazi Germany and seeing it as an early signpost on the road to fascism. Martin Barker's book on video nasties[2] took this approach and John Keane's book on the media and democracy fails to give credence to the theory and practice of state regulation.[3] I say 'blindness' advisedly for it is on the political left that the liberal-democratic emphasis on the 'individual' has been most criticised and if socialism still means anything it must mean something like the regulation of the means of production – and yet cultural production is frequently excepted. This is a major paradox.

Of course the left has traditionally given 'art' special consideration for artistic products have, particularly under modernism, been the spearhead of the critique of bourgeois social relations. But it doesn't take too much thought to realize that art is embedded in forms of cultural production which include, especially in the case of both film and reproduced film on video, large commercial interests and corporate planning. In the case of film, the United States hegemony is evident. If one examines the making of films, one soon realizes that the idea of the director as the author of the work is rarely the case and even the idea of a collective author must take into account the financial interests of backers, stars, marketing forecasters and so on. Films are frequently pre-cut to national markets, to the taste of preview audiences and so on. These points do not in themselves make a case for censorship, but they do raise questions about the authenticity of a free artistic market in terms of production and the possibilities of social regulation of different kinds, for example to make space for products of countries without the financial or cultural clout of the USA, a point made recently by a number of European directors. Britain is making fewer films and only television seems able to fund new low-budget and experimental work.

At the level of consumers, the market is similarly limited. Many films are just not available since distribution is orientated towards the new and to the products of the United States, with a dearth of repertory cinema in Britain and many European, east European and 'third world' films getting no chance of a release. On video the classics of world cinema are slowly being made available but one would still search in vain for Ozu, Dreyer, most of Bergman, Renoir and Weimar cinema and many others. Of course television screening, especially on Channel 4, provides a kind of idiosyncratic repertory, but advertising breaks provide their own kind of marketing intervention on the film narrative. In the words of the Russian film director, Andrei Tarkovsky, the art of film is 'sculpting in time'. The broadcasting of a work constructed according to the movement of sound and image through time is quite evidently a different kind of work when that sequentiality is interrupted at intervals by advertising breaks. Interpolation can be as problematic as censorship.

From the viewpoints of both production and consumption the market is seriously skewed and, owing to the expense of films, the advent of world markets, and the links with merchandising, the dominant trend is towards the mass market, Hollywood film. Rather than just face the market trend it is possible for governments to act to regulate markets in certain ways, for example to support local production, as used to happen with the EADY levy in this country, where a proportion of box-office receipts went towards a subsidy for the British film industry. The success of the Australian film industry since the 1970s is an example of government support. The case for social regulation is not just a prerogative of the left but would be admitted by Liberals and Conservatives: the crucial socio-economic point is not to collapse cultural production completely into commercial interests, but to see that it does not work according to some putative free market or emanate from a pure artistic spirit.

A Case for Censorship

A further point, which moves social regulation nearer the arena of censorship, is to admit that cultural production influences – albeit in complex ways – minds and bodies. The adamant Liberal might conjure up the notion of the autonomous, free-thinking individual who weighs all cultural processes quite rationally, but current theories of representation and the psyche would give this short shrift. The huge market of advertising shows the play of representation and motivation on the channelling and even the construction of desire.

To take this further, I would emphasize the specific nature of film and video images. They are iconic signs in the way that words are not. Though we know we are watching the result of light on celluloid or electronic images, we also know we are watching not only life-like figures but the traces of real people on the film or video screen. One of the marvels of the cinema is its kinetic quality and technological advances have made possible a large number of things to be seen to be done to the human body. The gangster, the horror and the sci-fi genres have been enabled to become extremely inventive, imaginative and violent. Iconic and kinetic depictions of the body are possible in film and video which are not possible in other cultural forms. But the use of identifiably real people can cause problems and there would be few I think who would want an unregulated market in, for example, depictions of children in sexual acts.

At this point one might distinguish between censorship and the law. Surely, it can be argued, the law can deal with extreme instances such as child pornography or real torture and so there is no need for the censor. Again, I would make necessarily brief arguments suggesting that there is a role for pre-publication censorship. First, the law on obscenity refers to 'the tendency to deprave and corrupt', implying a possible gradualism or incrementalism of some inclination to immorality. It is perhaps the repetition and familiarity of certain images that are a problem rather than one instance alone, for example the frequency in the 1970s of the rape-turning-to-consent scenario in certain kinds of pornography. The nature of the law in prosecuting specific works makes acknowledgement of this difficult. Second, the law, in acting post hoc, could be in the situation of closing the stable door after the horse has bolted. This is particularly true of video since video is so easily and cheaply accessible and copiable. Third, the fear of prosecution and the expense of litigation could work to make venturesome projects of film and video makers less likely to be funded. Fourth, evidence from court cases on obscenity suggests that the law takes a fairly primitive view of media aesthetics and, acting directly for a client, could be more cautious than a censorship body. An example is *Videodrome* (1982), cut on film on legal advice in 1983 but passed uncut by the Board on video. This suggests that a censorship body might be more liberal than a narrow interpretation of the law suggests and the censor's certificate can be an imprimatur, a form of protection for unusual works. It is arguable, for example, whether or not a lawyer, acting for a distributing company, would have recommended the passing of *Ai No Corrida* (1976), with its explicit erection, fellation and ejaculation shots, given the strictures of court views on the representation of these sexual acts.

So far I have argued a role for censorship, not a recommendation for extending censorship, but for its role in respect of certain public media. At the very least I hope I have suggested that there is a debate here. Certainly this indicates the kind of philosophical and ethical questioning with which the censor continually taxes him or herself. Of course if such a role is conceded in theory then it all depends on the particular practice within a certain media area. Almost all countries operate some kind of censorship and classification system for film and/or video. The British Board of Film Classification is unusual in Western Europe in not being a state organisation but one set up by the film industry to monitor itself. It is similar to the United States system in this respect and it is instructive to make some comparisons between the two.

Media policy in the United States has a clearer base-line since freedom of expression is enshrined in the constitution; and the role of the film censor is to classify rather than reject or recommend cuts. And yet there is a sleight-of-hand here for the 'X' category is known as a porn category and to give a mainstream film an 'X' rating rather than the usual adult category of 'R' is effectively to limit severely its commercial prospects. In practice then films are cut, in response to Board refusals, in order to achieve 'R' ratings. The US system puts a great emphasis on the role of parents since children can and do go and see 'R'-rated films, so long as they are accompanied by someone over 17. These include many horror films which are given '15' or more usually '18' in Britain. Also films like *Fatal Attraction* (1987) and *The Accused* (1988) were given 'R' ratings.

Recent cases, highlighted by the Spanish director, Pedro Almodovar, where one of his films – *Tie Me Up, Tie Me Down* (1990)

– was given an 'X' rating, showed how this system militated against foreign films dealing with sexual themes in unusual ways. For some time, it seems, the US Board has felt that the availability of the 'R' to children tended to weaken the adult category and they have now brought in a new category, 'NC17' which excludes children. The 'NC17' is close to the British '18'.

In the British system there is no clear constitutional safeguard for freedom of expression and perhaps there should be. Certainly there is a strong argument for a bill of rights. Yet declarations of rights are usually hedged with moral provisos – the United Nations Declaration and the EC legislation on the free market of goods are examples. The example of the United States shows that rights to freedom of expression do not guarantee any effective voice for minority views or seriously affect the domination of the media by corporate interests and consensus views.

The British System

The British Board of Film Censors, as it was called until the 1980s, was organised by the exhibitors in the film industry in 1912 to pre-empt the likelihood of a state censorship body. In the early years it was influenced by the Home Office and between the world wars took clear stances in restricting film discussion on political issues such as unemployment and civil strife. There was a limited liberalisation in the 1960s but it was not until the late 1970s that a coherent liberal credo was operated, based on the harm criterion and the need to justify intervention. Paternalism and the idea of film as purely for mass entertainment were dominant ideologies until the late 1960s and 1970s.

Before World War II some of the Russian films of Eisenstein were banned and there was a policy not to pass films which dealt with social issues such as industrial unrest. Even through the 1960s the censors frequently objected to what seem now like mild sexual references. But the rejection in the United States of the old Hays code, instituted in the early 1930s in response to Mae West and the gangster movies, made it clear that films could now become more explicit in both themes and treatment and it was inevitable that Britain would follow in the general movement towards cultural liberalisation at this time. Yet it would be facile to see this simply as progress despite the opening up of a much wider artistic repertoire, for there is some considerable truth in the idea of censorship as the mother of metaphor. The censor's dislike of viewing killing and victim in one shot in the gangster film of the 1930s gave rise to more sophisticated editing. And the sexual repressions and yearnings of films like *Suddenly Last Summer* (1959) and *Splendour in the Grass* (1961) in the late 1950s and early 1960s are now difficult to recapture when visual explicitness is the norm.

With the advance of media studies, the fragmentation of parts of an older paternalistic establishment and the advance of sociological studies, feminism and re-framings of political attitudes through the 1960s and 1970s, the modern censor is more likely to be a socially aware cinéaste than a moral guardian with a suspicion of mass culture.

In effect, the BBFC has two related functions, film and video. It should be noted that the first is theoretically limited in that it is local authorities who are the official licensing authorities for cinemas in their jurisdiction and that as such are empowered to disagree with BBFC classifications and give their own categories to individual films in the locality. This might go either way so that in the 1970s for example, the GLC gave 'X' (London) to *The Texas Chainsaw Massacre* (1974), though it was banned by the BBFC, while in the mid-eighties, just before its demise, the GLC became concerned at violence and sexual violence in the cinema, questioning though finally agreeing the '15' given to *Rambo* (1985) by the Board. *The Life of Brian* (1979) was banned by some authorities and *9½ Weeks* (1985) was restricted in Brighton.

In 1984 the BBFC became responsible for videos which were for sale or hire in Britain, using the same classifications as for film: U, PG, 15 and 18 with 'R18' as a classification restricting sale or hire to sex shops. Through the early 1980s there was considerable discussion about whether or not the wealth of new videos, many of them being versions of films not hitherto seen in this country, should be policed or not. This controversy rapidly polarised into scare stories on both the moral right – exaggerating the effect to which children were vulnerable – and the libertarian centre/left – positing state control of Orwellian proportions. Undoubtedly the

Video Recordings Act of 1984, giving responsibility to the BBFC to classify video works (with exemptions for education, music and sport) was more draconian that it needed to be, but it did not have the dire effects predicted by libertarians. On the moral right a cavalier use of evidence and a disdain for the art of the film exaggerated the problem, but on the left the denotation of moral panic evaded the real concerns about the problems of accessibility to children of certain media images and about the place of a new technology. As with the later Rushdie Affair, the camps had already been drawn and it was difficult, if not impossible, to suggest that such a polarisation was a simplification of the cultural politics involved.

At this point it should be said that most of the film censor's job is concerned with classification, not cutting or banning films. But there I am talking about the hard edge where the scissors might fall. The Board's primary duty is to the distributor, ensuring that what is passed does not fall foul of the law. This involves a duty to the audience, too, since the law reflects a regard for the effects of images. Guidelines are based on legislation. The main legislation is, of course, the Obscene Publications Act (1959, 1964), which first pertained to literature and was later extended to film works. There is other legislation, the Cinematograph (Animals) Act, 1937, forbidding cruelty to animals to be shown on the screen and, more recently, an act forbidding the sight of children in sexual scenes, the Protection of Children Act, 1978. The law on blasphemy is very occasionally relevant, as in the rejection of the video *Visions of Ecstasy* which was never released. In this instance the Board decided that the images of the sexual ecstasies of Saint Teresa and the involvement of Christ in these was made in a pornographic style rather than illuminating ecstasy or Saint Teresa in any way, a view upheld by the Video Appeals Board. The issue of criminal libel was raised in respect of *International Guerillas* (1990), the video portraying a man called Salman Rushdie being hunted down and killed. Here the argument of the Board was that in the specific naming of Mr Rushdie, the video presented a prima facie case for a libel prosecution. This view was rejected on appeal and Mr Rushdie gave notice that he had no intention to go to court on this. Other legislation might also be relevant, the law on hypnotism is a recent example. The Race Relations Act has also been used. It is also incumbent on the Board not to pass films or videos which might teach criminal techniques.

Sex and Sexual Violence

Since the 1970s the BBFC has had an explicit policy on sexual violence which entails cuts in, or even a rejection of films or videos in which sexual violence is presented erotically. This policy is most obvious when applied to traditional pornographic material, addressing a male audience, where a rape is presented explicitly either as a sexual turn-on or where rape is situated in the scenario as the appropriate way for women to achieve sexual satisfaction. Such a scenario might also appear in more mainstream material such as the women's prison genre or a thriller. It could be argued that such scenes can be considered obscene.

The Obscene Publications Act, though much criticised, is actually a fairly subtle piece of legislation, certainly much more so than the check-list revisions of the Act offered by recent private members' bills in the House of Commons. It defines obscene material as that which 'has a tendency to deprave and corrupt a significant proportion of the likely audience.' The heavy Victorian language of 'deprave and corrupt' sounds strange to modern ears but I would suggest the problem is really one of the poverty of our current language of morality. As Alasdair Macintyre argues in his book, *After Virtue*: 'we possess indeed simulacra of morality, we continue to use many of the key expressions. But we have – very largely, if not entirely – lost our comprehension, both theoretical and practical, of morality.'[3] While many on the left disdain moral discourse as the domain of the traditional right, all at some time become involved in pointing out various 'immoralities', whether these be of Government policies on housing, health or unemployment, of tortures and ethnic cleansing in Bosnia, royalty or press reporting, racism or even of censorship.

To be encouraged to find enjoyment in the suffering of others and to support this with ideological schema would seem to be clear instances of pleasures which might be described as 'corrupt'. The advantage of the phraseology of the Act is that it does not presume an identifiable and immediate modification of behaviour or thought by the viewing of, say, one eroticised act of rape, but speaks of 'a tendency', a gradual reinforcement of ideas identified with certain pleasures over time and through a series of viewing acts. It also specified 'the likely audience' which enables arguments on subjectivity to be sustained further and prevents obscenity being surmised on the basis purely of shock or offence. It also enables diverse subjectivities to be deployed in argument, so that a homoerotic video, for example, would have to be judged in relation to its likely homosexual audience. Lastly, the Act provides for the work accused of obscenity to be judged according to 'the work as a whole'. This provides for a whole poetics of film or video to be brought into play and prevents a scene or a visual being judged out of context. There is a public good defence which makes possible the publication of explicit material on the grounds of social or artistic worth.

Once one begins to look at pornography on an almost daily level, one realized that a simple pro- or anti-pornography stance is impossible. First, although the intention to sexual arousal might be a good working definition of pornography, such arousal does not imply necessarily the lone male masturbator. Second, pornography varies a lot, especially since the advent of video, which is now much more relevant than film pornography. Different types of pornography include: the standard North American hard-core, softer mainstream films of the *Emanuelle* (1974) kind, stripping, tapes, homosexual pornography of various kinds, bondage, 'female domination', leather and rubber specialities, transvestite and trans-sexual interests, large-breasted women, older women, wet clothing and bodies, adult male 'babies', spanking, foot fetishism and so on. And although pornography becomes defined by distribution, marketing and censorship patterns; the sex shop, the 'R18' or top shelf '18', the address to the proposed audience, there is also a strong sexually explicit element in many mainstream films.

In many of these the likely audience is fairly clearly gender-specific and most pornography featuring heterosexual sex activities (and mock-lesbianism) addresses males. To be honest, most of it is rather banal. The narratives are usually stereotyped and perfunctory, the acting poor and the sex scenes predictably the same. But there are some tapes which have good production values, are witty, comment on sexual mores or have aesthetic qualities which can go beyond their intended audience. Video technology has enabled both a significant change in production and the development of a variegated audio-visual sex market. Cheap to make, sex videos featuring amateurs and made by amateurs now proliferate, and specialist tapes can make a profit in a small niche market.

Britain is one of the strictest countries in Europe in its definition of the obscene. The differences among European nations indicate that a 'community censorship policy' is highly improbable. Holland is very liberal compared to Britain, France's classifications are far lower than Britain's, Sweden is most concerned with violence while Germany focusses on censorship for children.

In this country there is no space, even in the restricted sex-shop category, for hard-core pornography, since the sight of actual penetration and the sight of an erect penis is taken as straightforward evidence of obscenity in the rough-and-ready notion used in seizure and forfeiture orders under the Obscene Publications Act. This was not the intention of the Williams Committee, reporting in 1982 on pornography, which had recommended the availability of more explicit pornography in restricted premises. Even without the under-the-counter black market in hard-core, there will be some erosion of this strict policy as set by the courts and police with the ending of customs controls on imported pornography. There are also current and much debated exceptions to this policy, as instigated by the Board in its policy on sex education tapes. Here it is argued that a visible need in sexual therapeutics makes possible the showing of more explicit sexual activity. This is also the case in tapes offering advice on HIV and AIDS.

The Board passes video-tapes showing various kinds of sexual practices though not coprophilia, sex with animals, children, or outright sexual sadism or torture. Of course material of this kind rarely reaches the Board but there are exceptions. I recall being quite disturbed by the sight of a torture scene which looked as if it could be documentary, inserted into an otherwise inocuous soft porn film on video. The scene was not only shocking in its explicit

146

presentation of gross mutilation but appeared grotesquely so in its placing in a soft-core narrative as a turn-on for a main character.

A marginal and debatable area is sado-masochism. The Board's concern here is the way in which tapes depicting sado-masochistic activities might legitimate real harm in actual practices. Of course the notoriety of the 'Spanner' case, in which a number of men were involved in a video of apparently consensual mutilations, has highlighted the moral debate on how far people can be allowed to harm themselves in a free society. Given the subordination of many women in their private lives, my own emphasis would be on the potential worry of practices such as whipping or extreme bondage practised on women shown on video becoming more commonplace and heightening expectations that women should necessarily lend themselves to these activities. The Board always tries to distinguish the syle of S&M tapes in terms of the gender emphases, the element of play, of negotiation, etc. In terms of mainstream cinema and video, S&M figures significantly in films such as *Blue Velvet* (1986), *Love and Desire* (1991), *9½ Weeks* (1985) and in a recent Chinese film, *The Golden Lotus* (1985). *The Golden Lotus* I found difficult since it did explore an interesting historical narrative (based on a Chinese classic) involving relations between the sexes but features striking scenes of sadism directed at women which went beyond the demands of the theme and appeared to offer possibly dangerous erotic pleasures. Experienced Chinese examiners also found the film difficult to classify.

The challenges are to practise a censorship alive to unequal social relations and cultural diversity, a censorship which is aware of the importance of free expression within a modern democracy and the rights of the artist to explore difficult subjects, but which is also conscious of the striking hold that images can have on the imagination. The balancing of art and commerce, individual desire and power relations, freedom and regulation, is not easy, especially in a political environment which paradoxically exalts the free market, possessive individualism and only the fragmented appearances of morality.

Notes

[1] Geoffrey Wood, 'Frenzies of the Visible', *Economy and Society*, vol. 21, no. 1, February 1992; also 'The Regulation of Culture', forthcoming.
[2] Martin Barker (ed) *Video Nasties*, Pluto Press, London, 1984.
[3] John Keane, *The Media and Democracy*, Polity, London, 1989.
[4] Alasdair Macintyre, *After Virtue*, Duckworth, 1981, p2.

I would like to thank Kay Parkinson and Jeremy O'Grady for their useful comments on earlier drafts.

Porn, Perversion and Sexual Ethics

AVEDON CAROL

Our society is organized around reproduction; our lives are channelled toward making proper procreative partnerships, and our economic arrangements are set up to encourage interdependency within the reproductive unit of one adult male and one adult female. Consequently, a failure to replicate, or at least resemble, such an arrangement is frowned on by society. Sexualities that venture too far from the reproductive base are therefore labelled 'perversions'. Even where homosexual pairings are tolerated, they are expected to imitate monogamous, heterosexual family life and remain tied to the same values. Sexual acts or scenarios that do not make intercourse a goal or priority tend to be treated as unacceptable. The sex dualism allows us to pretend that men are unable to control their sexual impulses; it falls to women, then, to lure male sexual partners and then keep them tied to the reproductive unit – the nuclear family. We must tempt them into the web – but be careful not to tempt married men, or the wrong men, along with them.

It would be nice to believe that this kind of thinking disappeared with the advent of the women's movement, if not the 'sexual revolution', but the attitudes that forced women into these balancing acts still seem to be with us. Female sexual responsibility continues to have connotations of control of others – principally of male desire – and little to do with either our own desires or real interpersonal ethics. Worse still, what little is said about women's sexual fantasies most often supports the view that they are something we should feel guilty about.

Surely, in this age of AIDS, we should do everything we can to turn our old sexual assumptions upside down – after all, masturbation is safer than sex with someone else, and spanking doesn't exchange bodily fluids. Yet even as the death toll mounts, both the authorities and some feminists seem obsessed with suppressing solo and/or fantasy sexualities such as the use of porn mags, bondage, or sex that isn't based in 'relationships'. And while it may seem to make sense to encourage 'relationships' (defined as monogamous) above non-monogamous behaviour, in truth it sends us right back into the desperate search for something that closely resembles marriage; that is, women are once again being instructed to find a single partner as a protection against the evils of the world. The obsession with 'appropriate' relationships is precisely what leads women to tolerate abusive, dangerous and oppressive behaviour from partners. This hasn't provided a comfortable atmosphere for a thoughtful woman to consider her own sexuality, let alone its ethics.

We can be grateful that the gay community has turned the anger and pain of AIDS into a positive campaign to challenge the very assumptions on which our sexual dilemma is based. Safer sex may, to the more puritanically inclined, mean *less sex*, but to the gay community, as well as to the more liberationist among feminists, safer sex means more imaginative sex.

But acknowledging the possibility of a broader range of sexual possibilities is not, by itself, an answer to our dilemma. The acceptability of one sexual act or another has, for many women, just meant a greater likelihood that we may find ourselves under pressure to perform such an act with a partner. Since female sexuality has been defined as part attractive and part reactive – but not as *active* – a broader spectrum of possibility doesn't necessarily translate into a greater likelihood that our own needs will be met in a relationship or other partnered sex. For me, this means that female sexual ethics have to go back to the original demands of the women's liberation movement: that women should have both the right to suggest or accept sex, on the one hand; and that women have the right to refuse sex, on the other. These rules would have to be considered legitimate not only in terms of 'acceptable' forms of sexuality, but in a right to suggest, for example, 'kinky' or unusual sexual possibilities, or to have non-monogamous sex.

150

Traditionally, women have not been understood to have these rights. We were expected to wait to be propositioned and to refrain from sex of any kind unless the circumstances suited social prescriptions. Once, that meant refusing to kiss on the first date, and declining all genital sex until marriage – after which we were required to accept and tolerate all sexual advances from our husbands. Whether we felt desire for these acts was irrelevant to whether we were allowed or required to perform them. The grounds for acceptance and refusal have changed in recent decades, but this operates to women's benefit only when we throw *all* the old rules out – and if things go wrong, we are on our own. However, throwing out those rules is a necessity. Unless women are willing to take full responsibility for understanding our own desires and putting them into practice, it is pointless to complain that our partners (or acquaintances) demand what we don't want or fail to provide what we do want.

It is also pointless to complain about the particular acts being demanded instead of the fact that demands, rather than mere open suggestions, are being made at all. The arguments regarding demands from men are currently being grounded in misleading specifics – that a husband insisted on a *kinky* act, or that he brought home pornography and required imitation of what was in the magazine or video. A few sexist assumptions are inherent here: one, that women never desire 'kinky' sex; another, that no woman could ever find pleasure in trying out acts that have been brought to her attention through pornography. Moreover, the argument suggests that it would have been perfectly all right if no pornography had been involved and the husband had merely demanded that his wife drop everything to perform missionary-position intercourse she did not desire.

Such arguments take for granted male demands for conventional sex acts performed within 'acceptable' relationships – that's why it took until 1991 for the law in England to begin to acknowledge that marital rape should be a crime. They also hammer home the belief that men alone can want more imaginative or adventurous sex. The idea that women should tolerate, and be satisfied with, nothing more than copulation suddenly takes on an unaccustomed (for feminists) respectability when it is couched in these terms.

There is a bitter irony here. It has long been a classic feminist complaint that, while intercourse alone may be all right for some, it isn't always enough to turn most of us on. Many of us have been moving into investigations of pornography, lesbianism, sex toys, oral sex, SM, etc. in an effort to find our own sexualities. Although lesbianism and cunnilingus have become acceptable in some circles, most of the other alternatives have tended to remain 'perversions' in our perceptions – even within the feminist movement. In fact, some feminists have particularly stigmatized alternative approaches to sexuality. Suddenly, we are supposed to be satisfied with very traditional forms of sex within monogamous structures. And while we may be allowed to enjoy cunnilingus, it is often perceived as 'degrading' for women to perform fellatio.

It shouldn't be so difficult to acknowledge sex as a source of physical pleasure that should be stimulating and satisfying to all participants. The idea that men *or* women should sacrifice their own pleasure to that of a partner is odious; sex is not a service for an individual whose needs and desires are privileged. Surely the only ethical approach for us between partners, regardless of sexuality or gender, is to treat sex, whether within relationships or on a casual basis, as an all-for-all mutual exchange of pleasure. It is unnecessary to approach the satisfaction of males as something 'bad' that men should forfeit as a trade-off on behalf of female pleasure.

True sexual responsibility was an issue that could be ignored by a society that privileged reproduction over desire and pleasure. If the rules necessitated only reproduction, they necessitated only male orgasm. If women died in childbirth, that could be passed over as the will of God. Those who were beset with unwanted pregnancies or veneral disease had probably failed to accept the structure's demands for monogamy and control, so their deaths were unimportant. The whole picture falls apart once you start to see women's lives and pleasure as meaningful subjects. For that matter, seeing adults of either sex as something more than the means of reproduction puts the whole structure on shaky grounds.

We have to take responsibility for the way we conduct ourselves sexually, of course. At the simplest level, recognizing that all parties in a sexual act have a right to enjoy the act is a good start. It shouldn't be impossible for most people to agree to activities that both/all enjoy, and to stay away from acts which one participant doesn't want. All parties must also recognize that everyone has a responsibility for safety – don't take risks with unwanted pregnancies and diseases being passed around, and don't casually play around with potentially harmful activities without making sure you know what you're doing and won't be damaging each other. We should educate ourselves and act accordingly.

And we should be honest with ourselves about what we like and don't like, and then be prepared to convey this information to our sex partners, as well as finding out what they like and what activities can be shared with pleasure. Although some of us were raised to believe that men 'knew' what to do, or that nature would always take over, the fact is that we are all different and we can't expect our partners to read our minds about what we want. It's become almost trite to talk about honesty in relationships, but the fact is that we *aren't* usually that honest about what we like, even with ourselves. Often we are frightened to admit that we have certain feelings and desires; that has to stop if we are going to have responsible, ethical sexual behaviour. *But: it is never okay to coerce or intimidate others into sexual behaviour they don't want to engage in, and it is always legitimate to refuse to participate in undesired sexual activities.*

We can get our ideas from anywhere – they pop into our heads independently, or we hear them from our friends, or we find them in marriage manuals or pornography – but how we present them to our partners is all important; they should just be ideas, suggestions – *not* demands. I may be frustrated if a partner is unwilling to try out an activity I like, but that doesn't give me permission to insult them because they don't want to do it. Nor is it oppressive for a partner to mention an interest in (or show me pornographic pictures of) an activity I haven't previously expressed a desire for – as long as there is no pressure on me to engage in those activities. Being allowed to discuss something doesn't negate a right to refuse it. A lack of desire for an act is all the reason I need for refusing it; there's no imperative to dismiss it as 'perversion' before I can reject it as an option.

By calling some acts 'perversions', we over-privilege other acts; anal intercourse, masturbation, SM, or homosexuality *must* be rejected, but heterosexual intercourse becomes undeniable. If only the 'perverted' is forbidden, then anything not forbidden becomes compulsory. Our society has tended in the past to treat heterosexual intercourse as the compulsory activity, with the result that many women, and quite a number of men, have found sex utterly unsatisfactory and sometimes painful and demeaning.

Oddly enough, one charge sometimes lodged against pornography is that, according to pornography-effects researchers Dolf Zillmann & Jennings Bryant,[1] people who are shown pornography in psychology experiments express greater dissatisfaction with their existing sex lives. We don't know whether seeing sexual materials actually makes them more dissatisfied, more aware of their dissatisfactions, or simply more willing to express existing dissatisfactions; we do know, however, that many people do express disappointment with their sex lives without having to be shown pornography. Since this very lack of satisfaction has been such a frequent complaint from women – including most feminists – it seems strange that a willingness to acknowledge that disappointment is treated as a 'negative' effect of pornography by anti-porn feminists.

This evaluation seems to stem from a fear that if men acknowledge dissatisfaction with the sex they have with their current partners, they will be more likely to put pressure on women to satisfy them in new ways, or else they will seek satisfaction elsewhere. But it might be worth considering that women, also unhappy with their present sexual arrangements, might welcome a recognition that things aren't working. It is more useful for women to be willing to re-evaluate than it is to keep assuming that any change will be for the worse. Women may be surprised to find that many of the complaints men have are not dissimilar to the complaints women themselves have about 'traditional' sexuality. For example, some men have complained that post-coital hygiene gets women charging out of bed before they've had a chance to cuddle. Others have admitted that they miss the sort of sex they used to have as teenagers before copulation became standard to their sex lives – the extended snogging sessions were fun in themselves, not just a poor substitute for intercourse.

Looking at how sexism works to stifle and oppress us in sexual terms means looking principally at relationships between men and women, where the basis for our role expectations begins, but it would be a mistake to assume that all of these problems disappear between lesbians. Many people harbour the mistaken belief that when men are removed from the equation of interpersonal sex and relationships, we are suddenly treated to a vision of 'pure' female emotion, intellect, style and sexuality, unpolluted by the expectations of men or male-dominated society, and thus entirely different from those things our culture views as 'unsavoury' – the kinkier, more exploratory and carnal aspects of sex – as well as misunderstandings, power conflicts and exploitation. This is false of course; women are no less sexual, no less confused, and no less willing to take advantage of power (when we have it) than men. This is not merely because we have been brainwashed into accepting 'male values' that treat physical sex as acceptable and fun, as some anti-porn feminists would claim. If anything, the most dangerous patriarchal value we have to cope with is the belief that women are all the same and should therefore be able to expect identical sexualities in each other.

In the past 20 years, lesbians increasingly have felt pressure to conform to the same expectations within lesbian relationships that women already feel trapped into in heterosexual contexts: making our sexuality conform to a popular female stereotype. This pressure comes from parts of the feminist movement that instruct women to suppress certain sexual desires in order to promote what is seen as a politically desirable – purportedly 'feminist' – sexual structure. Women in general, and lesbians in particular, have been expected to exemplify the 'ideal' of a sexuality that devalues sexual adventure, 'perversion', and genital pleasure. Masturbation, particularly in the context of pornography, is defined as a 'male' (and therefore unacceptable) pleasure in this formula. (The emerging lesbian sex magazine market has been hit hard by this repressive 'feminist' philosophy: a feminist bookstore in North America was put out of business when anti-porn women organized a boycott because the store carried lesbian magazines; in Canada, a supposedly 'feminist' anti-porn law has found it's first victim in one such magazine.) Remarkably, anti-pornography feminists seem oblivious to how closely this formula resembles the traditional anti-sex instructions of the moral right. If women adhere to this design we will become indistinguishable from our anti-feminist predecessors who were also taught to turn up their noses at sexual pleasure. It is also, ironically, based on a logic that leads away from lesbianism, since there is no reason to make such partnerships at all if desire is unimportant. If sexual pleasure is unnecessary, what possible reason is there for sex that isn't procreative?

Most feminists agree – in the context of rape activism and on abortion – that women have a right to control our own bodies. This must mean that we also have a right to control our own sexuality, including masturbation, fantasy, role play, choice of partners, posing for or acting in pornographic materials, and using such materials. Any attempts to suppress these activities will directly oppress women, stigmatizing us, filling us with guilt, censoring our attempts to find out who we really are, returning us to the silence that allows our abusers to coerce us into undesired activities – activities which endanger us with infections, unwanted pregnancies, cervical cancer, and AIDS. Our freedom to investigate and to choose is not merely a search for some abstract idea of ethical sexuality – it is, for many of us, a matter of life and death.

Notes

[1] Dolf Zillman and Jennings Bryant, 'Effects of massive exposure to pornography' in N. Malamuth and E. Donnerstein (eds.), Pornography and Sexual Aggression, Academic Press, London, 1984.

Health, Education and Authority: Difference and Deviance

ROBERTA MCGRATH

'The knowledge we use on a daily basis continues to inform our action and inaction, our love and hate. It affects our chances of happiness and may determine our chances of survival'.[1]

The diseases of HIV and AIDS lie at the intersection of sexuality and identity, desire and subjectivity. The configuration of these diseases has inspired extremes of love and compassion, loathing and fear. If we have learned very little that is new about disease, we have learned much that is old about ourselves.[2]

HIV and AIDS are both ordinary and extraordinary. Ordinary because more than ten years into the epidemic we know that it has far more in common with patterns of other diseases than was previously thought. But extraordinary because of the ways in which AIDS has condensed social and cultural meanings about the late twentieth century. It has come to symbolise postmodernity. HIV is subtle and the diseases of AIDS devastating. They have tested our belief in scientific and human progress. There is no cure for AIDS, nor a vaccine against HIV.

In this chapter I consider the meanings of HIV and AIDS through an examination of the relationship between health, education and visual representation. But I want to begin by discussing the historical period into which the diseases of HIV and AIDS emerged. This a story about death, but it is also a story about survival.

HIV and AIDS appeared in 1981 in Britain and the United States at the beginning of a decade of moral crusades in both countries.

Moral panics 'emerge in complex societies when deep rooted and difficult to resolve social anxieties become focused on symbolic agents which can readily be targeted'.[3] Those agents were homosexuals, drug users, ethnic groups and women. If the eighties are to be remembered for anything then it will be as a decade which saw a marked increase in homophobia and racism, a backlash against feminism and a panic about sexuality which became the target upon which all those other anxieties could most easily focus.

The roots of this backlash lay in the seventies which had seen the formation of politically conscious black, feminist and gay groups. The latter two groups in particular forged their identities through sexual and cultural politics which acknowledged sexual differences as well as the power and pleasure of fantasy and desire. By the end of the decade theories of sexuality and subjectivity had become central to an expanded understanding of the relationship between the public, private and political. The personal had become politicised.

At the same time that AIDS was being identified, the visible power of feminist and gay groups was being perceived increasingly as threatening and dangerous to existing structures of society. A tension between emergent and established groups placed the sense of a coherent society under strain. 1981 was the start of a decade which eroded our sense of the 'public' and of 'society'. It was a period which increased the rights of powerful corporate bodies at the expense of the economic, legal, political and welfare rights of the majority of its citizens.

In Britain, as we live through another term of Conservative rule it is hard to estimate the social devastation and human damage caused by a decade of greed and indifference.[4] The 1980s were for most 'the worst years of our lives'.[5] On both sides of the Atlantic, public memory and history were relentlessly dismantled in favour of a competitive individualism coupled with a jingoistic nationalism. Many struggled just to survive; some did not.

With public health care systems that were ill-prepared and underfunded, governments were unable to deal with a disease of epidemic proportions. Science and medicine were unable to contain the threat which it posed.[6] It was a crisis.

158

Discourse and Language

'Language is not a substitute for reality; it is how we know it. And if we do not know that, all the facts in the world will not help us'.[7]

Discussion of HIV and AIDS is marked by an emphasis on facts and by recourse to scientific and research data which are presented to us through authoritative statements. This should alert us to a problem: facts are most usually invoked when they are most lacking and the voice of authority called upon when there is a crisis which is so threatening that it cannot be controlled.

Scientific discourse claims to be objective. This is the basis for its authority in claiming to describe the real. While it is important to stress that discourse is not a substitute for reality, it is equally necessary to acknowledge that we have no direct access to reality. Diseases, for example, do not refer to 'real' clusters of phenomena; they do not exist outside of the system and structures, the frameworks – scientific or otherwise – which give them meaning.

Writing in 1987 Paula Treichler argued that we needed not simply epidemiological information on HIV and AIDS, but an epidemiology of *signification*.[8] Others have commented that a great deal of social scientific research has been much less useful than it might have been precisely because of its emphasis on positivism and at the expense of more theoretically informed approaches.[9]

Language is about power; the power to define terms and to set the limits of what can and cannot be said. The biomedical discourse of disease cannot be separated easily from other discourses. The mass media have played a fundamental role in shaping what we think we know about the diseases of HIV and AIDS. Media representations are part of our understanding of what the diseases are. Early in the epidemic, even mainstream writers suggested that People with AIDS (PWAs) should avoid media coverage.[10] Others suggested that people were 'destroyed as much by the idea of AIDS as its reality'.[11]

But in our culture there is a hierarchy of knowledge. If language is about power, then it is also about privilege. Scientific language with its claims to objectivity and neutrality is a particularly privileged discourse. Biology is, for example, usually perceived to be the body itself; media representations are commonly seen as reflections, true or false, of a body which exists prior to those representations. But we

Steve Bell, 1986

should remember that these are both systems of representation; contiguous rather than innately hierarchical. 'Biology is not the body itself, but a discourse about the body'.[12]

The biomedical classification of HIV infection as a Sexually Transmitted Disease (STD) has had consequences for our understanding of the virus. It could and might have been classified differently. Horton and Aggleton cite Hepatitis B as a viral disease which is transmitted via exactly the same body fluids, blood and semen, as HIV.[13]

This has meant that HIV and AIDS has been understood as, first and foremost, an STD, (the archetype of which is syphilis). This classification profoundly affected both scientific and popular discourses and the management of the disease. Starting with the belief that HIV was transmitted via male homosexual intercourse, shifting later to the African sub-continent and to drug users, the discourse condensed and coalesced meanings about deviant sexualities, races and social behaviour in its search for the source of contamination. It consigned those who were already on the periphery to the category of the expendable.

Fears about social and cultural differences can most easily become focused on the human body which acts as a powerful metaphor for the social body. Virchow's cellular pathology in the nineteenth century viewed the cells in the body as a micro-model of the citizens within the body politic.[14] This has had repercussions in public health policies which have centred on the need for 'cordons sanitaire' in order to control disease. In the 1980s, the body took on a political significance which led to renewed demands for its regulation, its incarceration, quarantine and disposal.[15] AIDS has become a potent symbol for late capitalist society. HIV is a simulacrum of DNA – a copy of a genetic code for which there is no original – and is the first human retrovirus, a new breed of virus which converts DNA into RNA and back into DNA producing mis-information within cells. It appears to be a post-modern disease. It threatens to turn our immune system against us and produces a circulatory system which is more likely to cause our death than fight off illness.

Like all post-modernist discourse it owes everything to modernism and the power of the West: to capitalism and colonialism with its industrial and military might. It is dedicated to the preservation of centre over periphery which is, after all, its only guarantee of continued power.

HIV and the diseases of AIDS therefore have been mapped out largely in Western terms both globally and locally. Their 'natural' history has been studied mainly in homosexual men living in urban centres in first world countries.[16] Until recently women have been excluded. The World Health Organization's Global programme on AIDS still has no specific projects for women.[17] And the use of high-tech medicine in the third world may well, as some writers suggest, benefit the wealthy Westernised urban minority, whose lifestyles are closer to those in the West, rather than the majority of local urban or rural poor.[18]

Health Education in the Age of Privatisation: The British Experience

'In the absence of, at present, a vaccine or cure for AIDS, the single most important component of National AIDS programmes is information and communication'.[19]

161

This statement is a mark of the limits of science and medicine and makes clear the importance of education and information as a means of prevention. But what does this mean when knowledge and information have become privatised and commodified?

This section looks at what might be called the medico-moral politics of representation. If, as the above statement suggests, health information and promotion are the main means of controlling the epidemic then the principal body responsible for this in Britain is the Health Education Authority (HEA). The HEA describes its purpose as 'to lead and support the promotion of health, increasing knowledge and understanding of the contributing factors of health and disease'.[20] But this statement has its limits. Since its inception in 1927, as The Central Council For Health Education, material for teaching and publicity has been a central part of its programme. With the Education Act of 1944 and the formation of the National Health Service in 1951 the Health Education Council (HEC) was formed. The HEC operated until 1987 under the 'arm's length' principle, and was able to mount (albeit limited) criticism of government policies.

In 1980 the Black Report warned that the difference in health between those in higher social classes and those lower down the social ladder was widening. In 1987 the report was updated suggesting that the gap had widened over the previous decade. Attempts were made to stifle its contents which were believed to be politically damaging in an election year. In April 1987, the HEC was disbanded and reformed as the Health Education Authority. Its status was changed to that of a regional health authority; its chief executive appointed on a short-term contract and made directly answerable to, and under the control of, the Secretary of State for Health. This re-organization greatly increased Government control over the HEA's work.[21]

Although the first cases of AIDS appeared in 1981 in both the United States and Britain, no public health policy was formulated here until three years later. It is remarkable that government could believe that the disease was singling out particular groups. This is a measure of its indifference to an emergent epidemic which seemed to target groups on the margins of society and which were perceived as deviant.

162

By the mid-eighties indifference was replace by panic. The budget for education and prevention increased from £135,000 in 1985 to £20m in 1986.[22] That year's 'Don't Die of Ignorance' campaign targeted not those groups most affected by the epidemic, but the entire population. HIV testing became available in the same year and in January 1987 a leaflet was sent to every household in the country. The following year, a similar leaflet 'Understanding AIDS' was mailed to every home in the United States. This response was triggered by evidence that an epidemic, which had previously been confined to dispensable minorities, was spreading to the population at large. It did not simply spread. It was always there. It was outside the discourse merely because the framework rendered it invisible.

Advertising AIDS

The 1986-1987 campaign was widely criticised for its failure to give a clear message and in the light of this a second wave of advertising was mounted. What certainly distinguishes those adverts from earlier HEC material is their sophistication. This was due to increased budgets which enabled collaboration with public relations advertising agencies from the private sector. Between 1987 and 1990 some £12m was spent on mass media work. This constituted 40-50% of the HEA's total AIDS budget.[23]

To understand this material we need to be aware of the context of privatisation as well as increased control exerted over public institutions by government. It is not unreasonable to suggest that the HEA's campaign particularly between 1986 and 1989, had far more in common with adverts such as those that floated public utilities than with any educational programmes. When British Gas was privatised in 1986 and used the 'If you see Sid ...', strapline, a letter appeared in the press suggesting that the public money spent on the campaign would have been better spent on AIDS education and prevention. Since this was unlikely, the writer suggested that these adverts could at the very least have combined the promotion of shares with a safer sex message such as 'If you see Sid, tell him to use a condom'.

There is, of course, an obvious conflict of interest between the need for health education for public good and advertising as a private and competitive system. Markets require competition and this necessarily encourages closed information systems and secrecy. This is at odds with a health sector which has, until recently, sought to develop an ethos of openness in the development of integrated service planning and in ways of sharing good practice'.[24] It is worth noting here that the HEA does not have the remit for educating and promoting health amongst injecting drug users. This is undertaken by the Department of Health.[25] This division of responsibility is an example of a lack of integration in services and has had particular consequences for the HEA's focus on the HIV as a primarily sexually transmitted virus.

Commercial advertising is at odds with education because it 'locates its skills in personal persuasion rather than in social or economic forces'.[26] It aims at individual response rather than any sense of collective or social responsibility. State health education material generally fails to acknowledge that there are any factors other than individual 'choice' which affect our health. For a government dedicated to consumerism, and in a country where private consumption rose almost three times as fast as public spending between 1979-1990, advertising appeared to be the ideal vehicle.

While much of the HEA's information on the AIDS programme is restricted, one researcher who has had access to information records the conflict between those in public relations and those whose background was in health promotion. The 1988 campaign used the slogan 'AIDS, you know the risks, the decision is yours'. But even this compromise was only reached after much discussion. The advertising agency had proposed the slogan 'AIDS, your life is in your hands'.[27]

This reproduces the dominant view of disease as an asocial interaction between pathogen and host.[28] Such a view naturalises what is cultural; it eclipses social and economic inequalities as well as the inequalities of ethnicity, gender and sexuality. It is at best simplistic and, as many have pointed out, potentially fatal in relation to HIV and AIDS.

Moreover, 'one of the central tenets of health promotion is that intervention should avoid victim blaming', should be non-stigmatizing and non-stereotyping and that it should avoid high levels of fear and alarm.[29] We could be forgiven for thinking that the campaigns set out to do the reverse. If the 1986-1987 campaign generated fear and alarm, the campaigns that followed in the press in 1989-1990 used stereotypes which stigmatised and marginalised groups who had very little power.

Advertising as a system endlessly reproduces dominant structures, and stereotypes are therefore its stock-in-trade. 'In order for HIV education to be instrumental in modifying sexual behaviour – its ostensible aim – it will have to confront those very stereotypes and preconceptions, particularly about sex and gender, that advertising as a communication system upholds, exploits and reproduces'.[30] Sex has been utilised by advertisers to sell commodities over a long historical period. Since we live in a patriarchal society, sex is most commonly signified by the female body, preferably white, heterosexual, young and healthy.

There is a conflict here. Firstly, in health advertising there is no perceived commodity to buy. Secondly, for a government that had promoted 'family values' a problem emerges as to how to encourage safer sex without appearing to condone promiscuity or promote homosexuality. Public health education targeting those most at risk was at odds both with the state and the church. By 1987 the Government had introduced draconian legislation. The church's moral message promoted monogamy and heterosexuality.[31] Consequently the HEA's AIDS programme has a primary goal of 'minimising HIV transmission' but crucially 'without harmful social impact'. Additionally advertising should 'not be offensive to reasonable minded people'.[32] This, perhaps, makes clear the medico-moral politics of representation. It helps us to understand the lack of clear, practical guidelines on what constitutes safer sex and explains the adoption of veiled information. What we are presented with is certainly aesthetically sophisticated, but it is educationally weak. It also makes sense of the curiously serious and sexless nature of images used between 1989-1990 which suggested that the risk of contracting HIV outweighed the pleasures of sex.

This second wave of advertising sought to shift the ground of the earlier 'AIDS: Don't Die of Ignorance' campaign. It used the endline 'AIDS: You're as safe as you want to be'. Its new aims were enshrined in an AIDS 'Charter'. Since then charters, which do not provide any legally enforcible rights but suggest that rights are being extended, have appeared in all public institutions as funding and resources diminish. The 'charter' stated that:

'We believe that many have not yet recognised the potential scale of the AIDS epidemic. Instead, those with AIDS, particularly homosexual men, have been stigmatised, and AIDS has been portrayed as a disease associated with 'undesirable minorities'.[33]

Laudable though the intention of this is, the discourse which the campaign produced was rather different. The adverts addressed a white, heterosexual audience. Drug-users were not mentioned, partly because drug-use was not and still is not, part of the HEA's brief, and also because drug-users do not represent a socially cohesive group. Instead they appeared as part of 'undesirable minorities'. But even within the campaign, adverts aimed at homosexual men did not appear in the mainstream press. Positive targeting of an audience is important. On the other hand it is unjustifiable to exclude those groups when addressing a general audience and to suggest that they do not form part of society as a whole. This also challenged the Charter's declaration that 'AIDS is everyone's problem', and built upon the contamination theory that such groups are liable to corrupt and endanger others and therefore do not deserve representation. Jeffrey Weeks has argued importantly that to acknowledge sexual diversity (or, for that matter, any other diversity), does not make it a norm.[34] Indeed, such campaigns have served to reinforce all diversity and difference as deviance: sexual and social undesirables: gay men, lesbian women, young single women, blacks, drug-users, immigrants, those who are poor.

This territory of otherness has, of course, been historically established and could easily be re-mobilised. One signal example is the conflation of misogyny and homophobia. In the nineteenth century the figure of the prostitute as contaminator was common. In brothels she consorted 'with eight to twelve men in the same night'.[35] In the late twentieth century bath houses became the bordellos where gay men 'have sex twenty to thirty times a night'.[36] The female body generally, and the bodies of prostitutes in particular, were pathologised. Prostitutes, having crossed the boundaries between private and public, were perceived as

IF THIS WOMAN HAD THE VIRUS WHICH LEADS TO AIDS,
IN A FEW YEARS SHE COULD LOOK LIKE THE PERSON OVER THE PAGE.

Health Education Authority, 1988-89

Pleasure Principles

WORRYING ISN'T IT.

The virus that leads to AIDS is known as the Human Immunodeficiency Virus. Or HIV.

A person can be infected with HIV for several years before it shows any signs or symptoms.

During this time, however, it can be passed on, through sexual intercourse, to more and more people.

There are already many thousands of people in this country who are unaware that they have the virus.

Obviously the more people you sleep with the more chance you have of becoming infected.

But having fewer partners is only part of the answer. Safer sex also means using a condom, or even having sex that avoids penetration.

HIV infection may be impossible to recognise, but it is possible to avoid.

AIDS. YOU'RE AS SAFE AS YOU WANT TO BE.

FOR MORE INFORMATION OR CONFIDENTIAL ADVICE ABOUT AIDS, FREEPHONE THE 24-HOUR NATIONAL AIDS HELPLINE ON 0800 567123.

Health Education Authority, 1988-89

168

reservoirs of disease contaminating men. In our own time in a world where 'being fucked is seen as less than male'[37] homosexual men have been stigmatised and like prostitutes perceived as degenerate and dangerous. These histories are important to an understanding of the advertising campaign.

When the two-page advert posed the question 'if this beautiful woman had the virus that leads to AIDS, how will she look in a few years' time?', we expected to turn the page and see a grisly image of a woman who is a shadow of her former self: a living skeleton. Our expectations are formed partly by earlier 'documentary' photographs of before and after images of AIDS 'victims' which appeared in newspapers in the mid-eighties and showed how diseases visibly ravage the body. But these photographs were almost exclusively of men. This image also draws upon earlier eighteenth and nineteenth century engravings of the perils of syphilis (which is, after all, the model upon which HIV and AIDS have been based) and these were almost exclusively of women. This allows the contemporary photograph to trade upon earlier representations and invert them. When we turn the page and see that the woman looks exactly the same we know we are simultaneously in the same and also in a different territory. The fetishised face, the long hair, the jumper which falls off the shoulder are all signs of woman as a lure and seductress. (The photograph was taken by David Bailey who has specialised in commercial fashion and soft pornography). The advert makes us aware that she is possibly the harbourer not only of disease, but of certain death. The whole point is that we don't know. Female beauty as a mask that conceals all that is rotten has a history both in literature and visual imagery. The photographs here alert us to the invisibility of the disease. Moreover, if there are no visible signs, then everyone is a potential bio-hazard. Just one fuck could kill you. Significantly, it is not a picture of a man.[38]

Lastly, we also need to ask under what conditions is it a cause for concern, rather than celebration, that some years after contracting HIV the woman looks so well and healthy? For whom is it worrying? The point here is that the adverts were not aimed at those who were living with the consequences of HIV and AIDS and for that group the campaign was deeply offensive. Presumably, their HIV 'status' disqualified them as 'reasonably minded people'.

SEX FEELS BETTER
WHEN YOU'RE USING A CONDOM.

You had sex last night.

It was a wonderful experience.

You didn't bother with the condom. You thought it might ruin the atmosphere.

So how do you feel this morning?

Perhaps a little worried?

Well here's something to think about.

In Britain the number of people with AIDS is still on the increase.

And for every person with AIDS, we estimate there are around thirty with HIV.

Human Immunodeficiency Virus is the virus which leads to AIDS.

Someone can have it for several years and still look and feel perfectly healthy.

But through unprotected sex, they can pass the virus on to you.

If you choose to have sex (and remember it is your choice) a condom can help protect you.

Let's start again.

You had sex last night.

It was a wonderful experience.

You used a condom. You'd talked about it beforehand and both agreed it was the right thing to do.

Now how do you feel this morning?

What a stupid question.

AIDS. YOU'RE AS SAFE AS YOU WANT TO BE.

FOR MORE INFORMATION OR CONFIDENTIAL ADVICE
ABOUT AIDS, FREEPHONE THE 24-HOUR
NATIONAL AIDS HELPLINE ON 0800 567 123.

Health Education Authority, 1988-89

170

While everything in this image suggested the stereotype of the sexually experienced woman, the femme fatale, it had its obverse in a second image where we see a younger woman who is inexperienced in sex, and 'too embarrassed to ask him to use a condom'. Those stereotypes, the mature woman who has sexual knowledge and asserts that knowledge and the ingenue, the child who knows nothing are two sides of the same coin: Juliette and Justine.

In a letter to *The Daily Mail* in November 1989, Reginald Murley, a former president of The Royal College of Surgeons, and confidant of Margaret Thatcher, claimed that 'the handsome woman' in the AIDS advertisement was unlikely to get the disease unless 'she becomes a drug addict or allows herself to be buggered'.[39] Lord Kilbracken, whose parliamentary question about the number of heterosexual men who had first contracted HIV through vaginal intercourse (with a partner who had no other risk factor) revealed the low number of heterosexuals who had contracted HIV. For Murley and Kilbracken heterosexual AIDS was a myth and only those who indulged in 'deviant' behaviour were at risk. A spate of headlines appeared stating that 'normal' sex was safe sex.

The two adverts aimed at homosexual men (with photographs by Herb Ritts) appeared only in the gay press. This destination provided a sort of semiotic boundary which protected dominant heterosexual and government interests. The endline 'AIDS You're as safe as you want to be' was dropped. It was a further year until an advert aimed at bisexual men appeared.

1989 marked a turning point. Earlier in the year, Mrs Thatcher had vetoed a national survey on sexual behaviour because she feared intimate questioning would invade privacy and could, in her words 'taint' the government. A more plausible explanation is that the survey would show that sexual practice is much more diverse than the state will acknowledge. Doctors and health professionals believed that the survey was crucial to prevention. Later the programme was funded by Wellcome who, as one of the wealthiest pharmaceutical companies and the manufacturers of Retrovir, stood to benefit from research. Between 1987 and 1990 Wellcome made over £200 million from a drug which was used originally to treat cancer. It was dropped because of its toxicity and lack of success.

The Government special cabinet committee on AIDS set up in 1986 was disbanded and by the end of the year the HEA had announced its plans to dissolve its separate directorate for AIDS.[41]

In 1990, as a result of this crisis in authority, there was a return to the opinions of 'experts' and the use of personal testimony from those living with HIV.

In the same year the Terrence Higgins Trust (THT) produced their 'Get Set for Safer Sex' poster series which utilised the conventions of advertising. Unlike the HEA campaign however, the message was that sex was erotic and pleasurable, and sexual practice diverse. They provided information on what constituted safer practice. This was very different from the Government's message. Research on the 1988 campaign had shown that 94% of those interviewed believed that sex was an important part of most people's lives. The report drew the conclusion that 'we should be telling them how to make it safer, not give it up'.[42]

This statistic points towards the contradiction between the objectives of health education and government policy. The Conservative government had propagated the view that promiscuity in particular was the cause of AIDS according 'the moral category of promiscuity a pseudo-medical status'.[43] This is the heart of the problem. Those measures which are most effective in preventing the spread of HIV are at odds with the moral stance of the State. Health promotion policies in connection with drug use are a prime example of this. Perl comments that 'free needle exchange which may most effectively prevent HIV infection, is not wholly compatible with government policy of preventing injection and stopping drug use as a whole'.[44] The Department of Health's campaign on drugs used fear and shock tactics. This model of health education, based on a much older idea of phobic avoidance, is generally recognised as unsuccessful. In the case of one of the campaigns, which showed injecting equipment, it was actually counter productive. Some drug users reported that the images of needles stimulated a desire to inject. For them the images were positively attractive.[45]

Perhaps what is important here is the instability of meanings which cannot be fully controlled by the producers, or contained by the structures within which they are placed. They depend, ultimately, for their meaning upon viewers. I would argue, that contrary to popular opinion, the meanings of photographs are particularly unstable. Photographs, perhaps more than other means of visual representation, seem to pin down and fix meaning. Photography appears to have a privileged relationship to the reality it depicts and which is the primary referent of all representation. As other writers have pointed out, what is produced through the product of that reference is realism – a discourse, not the real itself.[46] This is as true for photography as it is for other cultural forms. Because photography reproduces many of the conditions of perception, and give us so much to see, it tends to blind us to its coded view of the world. As the 'handsome woman' in the advertisement demonstrates, meaning is never innocent. Any realist image works by a controlled and highly limited recall from a reservoir of images that already exists. The means through which the image is produced are effaced. The view of the world it presents is selective and constructed, but is made to appear natural through a constant repetition of images, gestures, lighting, angle and so on which produce what we recognise as 'real'. This is a world which is seamless and internally free of contradiction. Most photographs, and particularly photographs used in advertising, conform to dominant ideologies. They confirm rather than challenge existing beliefs about the world. The trick of advertising is to make it appear as if everything is changing, when in fact everything stays the same.

Counter Strategies

The censorship inscribed in Section 28 in this country and the Helms' Committee Report in the US, introduced to repress gay and lesbian activity, united these communities in a renewed wave of political and cultural action. This is perhaps best summed up in Act Up's 'Silence=Death' sticker which is an example of 'reverse discourse'.[47] This makes it possible to appropriate and reverse pathological definitions. Used transformatively, another vocabulary can be produced. Those discourses that oppress, silence and marginalise, also give voice to, and provide a means to speak and to articulate a very different discourse. This has produced a politics not just of resistance, but of transgression.

Dominant discourse has defined homosexuality as an identity

Pleasure Principles

HE'S INTO SAFER SEX, SO WHY NOT GIVE HIM A HAND?

It's a scene you may already be familiar with. Your eyes meet across a crowded pub and before you know it, you're away.

He may have swept you off your feet but hopefully you'll still remember those two little words, 'safer sex'.

More and more people now know that anal intercourse carries the greatest risk (for either partner) of transmitting HIV, the virus that causes AIDS. Even using a condom doesn't make it completely safe.

So you should expect your new friend to be into things like mutual masturbation, fingering, massage and rubbing his body against yours.

Even oral sex can be on the menu, assuming of course, that he has no cuts or sores in his mouth and does not swallow semen.

You'll find more details on the fact cards which are posted up around clubs and bars.

It's a matter of adopting a fresh, positive and imaginative approach to sex.

So shouldn't you have a hand in it?

Health Education Authority, 1991

HOW FAR WILL YOU GO BEFORE YOU MENTION CONDOMS?

THIS FAR?

THIS FAR?

THIS FAR?

THIS FAR?

Today, no one can ignore the need to mention condoms. Have sex with someone without using one and not only could you risk an unwanted pregnancy, but you also risk contracting one of the many sexually transmitted diseases.

Like Herpes, Chlamydia, Gonorrhoea, and of course HIV, the virus which leads to AIDS.

So the question isn't if, but when you mention condoms. You could mention them at any moment leading up to sexual intercourse. In reality, it's not quite so easy.

Mention them too early and you might feel you look pushy or available. Leave it too late and you risk getting so carried away you might not mention them at all.

When is the easiest moment to say you want to use one? How about while you're still wearing your knickers? In this instance it would be picture three.

By now you've gone far enough to make it obvious that you both want to have sex. But not so far that you're in danger of getting emotionally and sexually carried away.

It's a perfect opportunity. So take it. Say you want to use a condom.

Say he hasn't got one? Well have one of your own at the ready just in case. It really doesn't matter whose you use.

And then you can go just as far as you like.

Health Education Authority, 1992

174

shaped by 'deviant' sexual practices and nothing else. Gay activist politics have not rejected that definition which at least acknowledges the power of sexual practice. But it has also re-defined that identity as one which is shaped by ideological and political beliefs: a cultural identity rooted in a particular historical moment. Stuart Hall defines cultural identities as 'the names we give to the different ways we are positioned by, and position ourselves within the narratives of the past'. Language and discourse does position us, and does indeed seek to fashion us 'in its own image'; but it also enables us to position ourselves; to contest meanings about who we are.[48] Cultural identities are therefore about shared experiences and interests and they are also, equally, about political alignments with specific aims and objectives.

It is within this context, the context of self-realisation through self-representation, that we should view oppositional strategies in health education. This takes us beyond the limits of photographic realism. Recent HEA material may have acknowledged that a diversity of races live in Britain. They have made sex look more pleasurable and the captions have changed from the old 'The more partners you have, the greater the risk' to the more collective 'Sex, we all know how much we enjoy it ... that doesn't mean no more sex ... but it does mean taking more care'.[49] The dominant ideologies of the advertising system, particularly of gender and race, seem to be so deeply inscribed within those texts that to many, especially women and people of colour, the most recent campaign can only appear as offensive and patronising. It is a reminder that advertising and education have a history of reproducing dominant power relations.

Therefore in the field of HIV and AIDS, peer education has not simply been an addition or adjunct to dominant state health education. It has been at the forefront providing much needed information about how to make sex safer. In 1990 the THT 'Get Set for Safe Sex' series generated a great deal of interest and drew attention to the trust's widening policies. Although originally set up to meet the needs of gay men, the THT has provided health information and support for other groups.

The most recent campaign, 'Tales of Gay Sex' (1992), rejects the seamless world of photographic realism and the high quality art

Pleasure Principles

Terrence Higgins Trust, 1991-92

176

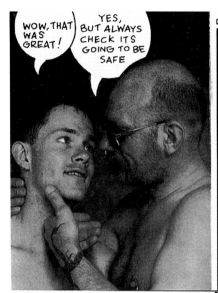

...to safer sex

There are two main ways in which you can
give or get HIV :

- by getting infected blood or cum into the
  bloodstream (for example, through sharing
  needles)
- by getting infected blood or cum up the arse
  or down the opening of the dick (by fucking
  or getting fucked)

Getting cum in your mouth is thought to be
very low risk.

Telephone the Terrence Higgins Trust Helpline on
071-242 1010 (3pm -10pm daily), for confidential
advice, counselling or information.
The Terrence Higgins Trust, 52-54 Grays Inn Road,
London WC1X 8JU. Registered Charity no. 288527
© The Terrence Higgins Trust 1991 Photographs by Jean-Marc Prouveur

Terrence Higgins Trust, 1991-92

production values of advertising. These leaflets are not designed for the press, but for direct distribution amongst the gay community. Content is not subordinated to style. The production values are low-tech and have more in common with the photo-stories of teenage girls' magazines. It mobilises popular forms to very different ends. These leaflets with their combination of photographic narratives and speech bubbles celebrate diversity in sexual practice – from masturbation to bondage and fucking.

The 'tales' which the photo-stories use are totally clichéd and the images are obviously, and crudely, montaged. But the humour combined with clear, practical information is a powerful incentive to practise safer sex. As one character says, 'It's better to have safe sex with a hundred guys than to fuck once without a condom'.[40] Another example which utilises bondage at least acknowledges that some sexual practices which have been stigmatised as deviant are amongst the safest. This cannot and must not be encouraged by the state's medico-moral politics and does not exist in HEA literature (especially for heterosexuals). As Donna Minkowitz has suggested, 'the vista of infinite sexual possibilities beyond the exigencies of procreation scares the family values posse more than anything'.[52]

Conclusion

It would be mistaken to end with the view that advertising as a system cannot be used to educate. Some of the most innovative work in this field has come from the United States which has seen a decade of culturally-based political activism on the streets. These images are a testament to collective social action. Nothing equivalent has existed here.

Advertising certainly cannot give detailed information, but outside of corporate and government interests it can ask questions. These are pictures which harness and then subvert the power of dominant advertising. They use the tools of advertising not to reproduce existing power structures, but to challenge them. The messages here are not about social status but about social injustice; these are texts which question dominant beliefs and give voice to groups who are marginalised and whose voices are not heard in public address systems. Most importantly of all, they make us aware

SEXISM REARS ITS UNPROTECTED HEAD
MEN USE CONDOMS OR BEAT IT
AIDS KILLS WOMEN

Gran Fury, 1990 (Billboard)

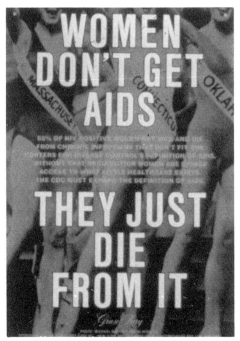

WOMEN DON'T GET AIDS

THEY JUST DIE FROM IT

Gran Fury, 1991 (Bus shelter poster)

179

Pleasure Principles

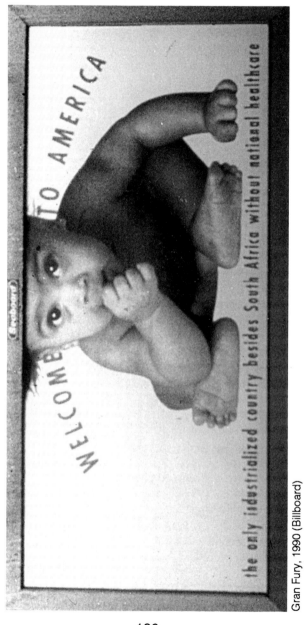

Gran Fury, 1990 (Billboard)

180

that the discourses of HIV and AIDS have shored up dominant ideologies at the expense of whole sectors of the population. The images reproduced here draw attention to the marginalisation of women. The history of HIV and AIDS might have been different. 'If history has a role to play in the present AIDS crisis, it is to restore public memory about our behaviour during past epidemics and to continue to raise questions about the meanings and consequences of disease'.[52] Public memory, social history and collective political action were disdained during the 1980s. These were incompatible with the corporate greed of privatisation which battled to narrow our minds and destroy our identities. These images are powerful because they raise question in the public arena about meaning and identity; about life and death. They remind us that a collective cultural politics of resistance is possible.[53]

Notes

[1] S. Harvey, 'Who Wants to Know What and Why?', *Ten:8*, no.23, p27.

[2] F.C. Tilney M.D., on the polio epidemic of 1916 in New York, quoted in E. Fee and D. Fox, (eds), *AIDS: The Burden of History*, University of California Press, Berkeley 1988.

[3] J. Weeks, 'AIDS: The Intellectual Agenda', in P. Aggleton et al (eds), *AIDS: Social Representations and Social Practices*, Falmer Press, Lewes 1989, p5.

[4] Gran Fury, 'Kissing Doesn't Kill; Greed and Indifference Do', *Poster* 1989.

[5] B. Ehrenreich, *The Worst Years of Our Lives: Irreverent Notes from a Decade of Greed*, HarperCollins, New York 1990.

[6] See R. Goldstein, 'The Implicated and the Immune: Responses to AIDS in the Arts and Popular Culture', in D. Nelkin et al (eds), *A Disease of Society: Cultural and Institutional Responses to AIDS*, Cambridge University Press 1991.

[7] P. Treichler, 'AIDS, Gender and Biomedical Discourse: Current Contests for Meaning' in E. Fee and D. Fox, *op.cit.*, p196.

[8] P. Treichler, 'AIDS, Homophobia and Biomedical Discourse: An Epidemic of Signification', *October*, no.43, Winter 1987, p68.

[9] J.D. Halloran, 'What can be Learned from the Evaluation of Health Education Campaigns and Programmes and from the Field of Mass Communication Research', in *Promoting Sexual Health: Proceedings of the Second International Conference on the Prevention of the Sexual Transmission of HIV and Other Sexually Transmitted Diseases*, British Medical Association and Health Education Authority, London 1991, p1.

[10] D. Miller, *Living with AIDS*, Macmillan, Basingstoke, 1987, p105.

[11] S.L. Gilman, 'AIDS and Syphilis: The Iconography of Disease', *October*, no.43, Winter 1987, p88.

[12] D. Haraway, 'Cyborgs at Large', in C. Penley and A. Ross (eds), *Technoculture*, University of Minnesota Press, Minnesota, 1991, p5.

[13] M. Horton and P. Aggleton, 'Perverts, Inverts and Experts: the Cultural Production of an AIDS Research Paradigm', in P. Aggleton et al (eds), *op.cit.*, p76.

[14] See Gilman, *op.cit.*

[15] These measures have included, in this country, the Public Health (Control of Disease) Act 1985 which allows hospitals to forcibly retain a person with AIDS who is thought to be a danger to others. In the United States in 1986 Proposition 64 requiring compulsory screening and mass quarantine in desert camps was put to voters in California. It was rejected. *Science*, no.17, October 1986, pp277-8. See also C. Patton, *Sex and Germs*, South End Press, Boston 1985.

[16] See B. Schneider, 'AIDS and Class, Gender and Race Relations', in J. Huber and B. Schneider (eds), *The Social Context of AIDS*, Sage, London 1992.

[17] C. Patton quoted in K. Bird and S. Thomas, *A World United against AIDS: VIIth International Conference on AIDS: A Summary*, Health Education Authority National HIV Information Service, London 1992.

[18] R. Frankenberg, 'One Epidemic or Three? Cultural, Social and Historical Aspects of the AIDS Pandemic', in P. Aggleton et al (eds), *op.cit.*, p22.

[19] Article 4, London Declaration on AIDS Prevention, World Summit of Health Ministers, London, January 1988.

[20] 'The Health Education Authority: What it is and What it Does', HEA Publications, London 1990.

[21] See The *Independent*, 25 March 1987, p1.

[22] J. Weeks, 'Love in a Cold Climate', *Marxism Today*, vol.31, no.1, pp12-17.

[23] S. Perl, 'Reflections on using Mass Media for AIDS Public Education', HIV/AIDS and Sexual Health Programme, Paper 13, Health Education Authority, London 1991, p5. The HEA has worked with the agency BMP DDB Needham since 1987. They have produced campaigns for Barclaycard, Stella Beer, War on Want amongst others.

[24] Editorial, 'Markets and Marketing', *Critical Public Health*, vol.3, no.1, 1992, pp2-3. See also, T. Rhodes and R. Shaughnessy, 'Compulsory Screening: Advertising AIDS in Britain 1986-89', *Policy and Politics*, vol.18, no.1, 1990.

[25] See Perl *op.cit.*

[26] K. Wellings, 'Selling AIDS Prevention', *Critical Public Health*, *op.cit.*, p10.

[27] *Ibid.*

[28] See J. Comaroff 'Medicine, Symbol and Ideology', in P. Wright and A. Treacher (eds), *The Problems of Medical Knowledge*, Edinburgh University Press 1982, p59.

[29] Wellings *op.cit.*, p7.

[30] T. Rhodes and R. Shaughnessy, 'Compulsory Screening: Advertising AIDS in Britain 1986-9', *Policy and Politics*, vol.18, no.1, 1990, p56.

[31] See Clause 28 of the Local Government Act 1988, and the first Vatican Conference on AIDS, 1989, which stated that 'the truth is not in condoms or clean needles. These are lies ... good morality is good medicine'.

[32] Perl, *op.cit.*, p5.

[33] AIDS Charter, Health Education Authority, London 1989.

[34] J. Weeks, *op.cit.*

[35] Frank Mort, *Dangerous sexualities: Medical-Moral Politics in England since 1830*, Routledge and Kegan Paul, London 1987, p214.

[36] Leo Bersani, 'Is The Rectum A Grave?', *October*, no.43, Winter 1987, p211.

[37] J. Minson, 'The Assertion of Homosexuality', *m/f* no.5/6, 1979, p74.

[38] There is one image of a man alone which the Health Education Authority interpreted as suitable for mainstream distribution as it could be addressed to either women or gay men. Significantly, it did not focus on the face.

[39] R. Murley, the *Daily Mail*, 7 November 1989, p6.

[40] M. Fumento, *The Myth of Heterosexual AIDS*, Basic Books, New York 1989.

[41] See the *Sunday Correspondent*, 21 January 1990.

[42] 'An evaluation of the Health Education Authority Public Education campaign, February-June 1988', Health Education Authority and British Market Research, London 1988.

[43] Rhodes and Shaughnessy, *op.cit.*, p29.

[44] Perl, *op.cit.*, p14.

[45] L. Sherr, 'Fear Arousal and AIDS. Do Shock Tactics Work?', in *AIDS*, vol.4, no.4, 1990, pp361-4.

[46] See J. Tagg, 'The Currency of the Photograph', in V. Burgin (ed), *Thinking Photography*, MacMillan, London 1982.

[47] This is an example of the appropriation of the Nazi symbol for homosexuality which was used to stigmatise. It is used by that group to define identity. On reverse-discourse see M. Foucault, *The History of Sexuality*, Penguin, Harmondsworth 1984.

[48] See S. Hall, 'Cultural Identity and Cinematic Representation', *Framework*, no.36, 1989, p69, and J. Grover, 'Dykes in Context: Some Problems in Minority Representation' in R. Bolton (ed), *The Contest of Meaning*, M.I.T. Press, Cambridge, Massachusetts 1989.

[49] Health Education Authority Advert, 1991.

[50] Tales of Gay Sex, 'Keep Them Coming with Safer Sex', Terrence Higgins Trust, p17, 1992.

[51] D. Minkowitz, 'Kids 'R' Us', *Village Voice*, 15 September 1992.

[52] G. Risse, 'Epidemics and History: Ecological Perspectives and Social Reponses', in E. Fee and D. Fox, *op.cit.*, p58.

[53] These images were first shown in this country at Tramway in Glasgow, October-December 1992.

I am grateful to Steve Bell, the Health Education Authority, the Terrence Higgins Trust and Gran Fury for permission to reproduce illustrations.

Pleasure Praxis

BE PLEASURED, BE PRINCIPLED, BE POLITICAL

ACT UP (London)
AIDS Coalition to Unleash Power
BM Box 2995
London WC1N 3XX
Tel 071 262 3121

Through forms of civil protest and direct action, ACT UP seeks to promote human rights for people living with AIDS and HIV, an end to discrimination in prisons, housing and employment, appropriate public education and information and an end to government complacency.

Black HIV/AIDS Network (BHAN)
106-108 King Street
London W6 0QU
Tel 081 741 9223

BHAN provides information, education and training and a buddy scheme for Asian, African and Afro-Caribbean people affected by HIV/AIDS.

Blackliners Help Line
Unit 46, Eurolink Centre,
49 Effra Road, London SW2 1BZ
Tel 071–738 7468 (Admin)/738 5274 (Helpline)

A counselling, drop in service, buddying and training and support for people with HIV/AIDS from Africa, the Caribbean and Asia who are living in Britain.

Body Positive
51b Philbeach Gardens
London SW5
Tel 071 835 1045

A self help information and support group for people affected by HIV/AIDS. Body Positive Women offers support, advice, complementary therapies and information for women living with or affected by HIV/AIDS.

British Board of Film Classification
3 Soho Square
London W1V 5DE
Tel 071 439 7961

BBFC is an independent non governmental body which has for over eighty years exercised responsibility over cinema, which by law belongs to local authorities, and since 1984, over the classification of videos.

Campaign against Pornography (CAP)
96 Dalston Lane
London E8 1NG
Tel 071 923 4303

CAP takes action against the pornography industry. It aims to raise awareness of pornography through campaigns, research and nationwide talks.

Campaign against Pornography and Censorship
PO Box 844
London SE5 9QP

It campaigns for the elimination of pornography, and aims to increase awareness and promote sex discrimination based legislation.

Campaign for Press and Broadcasting Freedom
Women's Section
7 Adelphi Road,
Epsom, Surrey KT17 15B
Tel 0372 745 903

English Collective of Prostitutes
PO Box 287
London
NW6 5QU
Tel 071 837 7509

A network of women of different races and nationalities working at various levels of the sex industry.

Family Planning Association
27 Mortimer Street
London
W1N 7RJ
Tel 071 636 7866

Information on family planning and contraception.

Feminists Against Censorship
BM Box 207
London WC1N 3XX
Tel 081 552 4405

A network of women campaigning against censorship from a feminist perspective.

Gay Men fighting AIDS
Unit 42, Eurolink Centre,
49 Effra Road, London SW2 1BZ
Tel 071–738 3812

Involved in HIV/AIDS campaigning and education with, for and on behalf of gay men.

Health Education Authority
Hamilton House
Mabledon Place
London WC1H 9TX
Tel 071 383 3833

A statutory agency responsible for health promotion.

HEA National HIV Prevention Information Service
82-86 Seymour Place
London W1H 5DB
Tel 071 724 7993

Provides a national enquiry and referral service for people with a professional interest in HIV education and prevention.

Lesbian and Gay Employment Rights (LAGER)
St Margarets House
21 Old Ford Road
London E2 9PL
Tel 081 983 0696

Information, advice, support and crisis intervention for lesbians and gay men, on anything affecting lesbian and gay men in employment. Specifically for queries in the area of employment.

London Lesbian and Gay Switchboard
Tel 071 837 7324

A 24-hour helpline offering advice, information and referrals on the whole range help available to lesbians and gay men.

Liberty (formerly National Council for Civil Liberties)
21 Tabard Street
London SE1 4LA
Tel 071 403 3888

A civil liberties organisation which aims to promote and defend civil liberties in the United Kingdom.

London Lighthouse
111/117 Lancaster Road
London W11 1QT
Tel 071 792 1200

Residential and support centre which aims to provide an integrated range of services to meet the needs of people affected by HIV/AIDS.

National AIDS helpline (24 Hour service)
Tel 0800 567 123

National AIDS Trust
6th floor, Eileen House
80 Newington Causeway
SE1 6EF
Tel 071 972 2845

An independent voluntary sector development agency concerned in all aspects of AIDS, other than medical research.

Outrage
c/o London Lesbian and Gay Centre
67-69 Cowcross Street
London
EC1M 6BP
Tel 071 490 7153

A non violent direct action organisation which campaigns for lesbian and gay rights.

Positively Women
5 Sebastian Street
London EC1V OHE
Tel 071 490 5501

Support, counselling and advice and information for women who have HIV infection or AIDS.

Stonewall
2 Greycoat Place
London
SW1P 15B
Tel 071 222 9007

An independent lobby group working for legal equality and social justice for lesbians and gay men.

Terrence Higgins Trust
52-54 Grays Inn Road
London WC1X 8JU
Tel 071 831 0330 (Admin)/242 1010 (Helpline 12 noon – 10pm)

Provides welfare, legal and counselling help to people with HIV/AIDS and related conditions, and to their friends and families. Disseminates information to the general public, policy makers and the media, provides health education and encourages, supports and assesses research into HIV/AIDS and related conditions.

The All-Parliamentary Group on AIDS
1 The Abbey Garden
Great College Street
London SW1P 3SE
Tel 071 219 5761

The role of the All-Party Group on AIDS is to raise awareness in Parliament and to encourage balanced policies based on accurate information. It aims to act as a Parliament and the statutory and voluntary sectors providing a forum for the exchange of information.

The groups listed are closely related to the material covered in the book. It is not intended to be an exhaustive list, but a glimpse at possible political practice. It is to inform, encourage and inspire. For more information on HIV/AIDS services contact the National AIDS Manual on 0717 371 846. For information about US based groups, for example Queer Nation, contact the Information Service at the National Lesbian and Gay Taskforce, Washington on 0101 202 332 6483.

Get out there – put the pleasure into politics.

Biographical Notes

Avedon Carol is a former singer and women's health counsellor who lives, writes and edits in London. She is a founding member of Feminists Against Censorship, a member of the Executive Committee of the National Council for Civil Liberties ('Liberty') and the co-editor of *Bad Girls and Dirty Pictures: The Challenge to Reclaim Feminism*, (Pluto Press, *London*, 1993).

Sue Golding is a Doctor of Philosophy and teaches at the University of Toronto. She is renowned for her work on Gramsci.

Della Grace is a photographer and author of *Love Bites* (éditions Aubrey Walters, 1991).

Victoria Harwood teaches Women's Literature at City University. She was an original organiser of the *Body Politic/Erotic Self* Conference and has helped organise many other conferences on the left. She still believes in 'loving nobly' and spends a lot of time trying not to fall in love with unsuitable types and watching Inspector Morse reruns.

Isaac Julien is a film-maker. His films include *Looking for Langston* (1989), *Young Soul Rebels* (1992) and *The Attendant* (1993).

Jackie Kay was born in 1961 in Edinburgh and brought up in Glasgow. She won an Eric Gregory Award for *The Adoption Papers* in 1991. Her first play, *Chiaroscuro*, was presented by Theatre of Black Women in 1986, and her second, *Twice Over*, by Gay Sweatshop in 1988. Her television work includes films on pornography, AIDS and transracial adoption, and *Twice Through the Heart*, a poetry documentary for BBC 2. *Other Lovers*, a collection of poetry is forthcoming (Bloodaxe, 1993).

190

Preface

Kenneth McKinnon is Professor of Film Studies at the University of North London. He has written a number of books including *Hollywood's Small Towns* (Scarecrow, 1984), *Misogyny in the Movies: the De Palma Question* (University of Delaware, 1990) and *The Politics of Popular Representation: Reagan, Thatcher, AIDS and the Movies* (Fairleigh Dickinson, 1992). He is currently working on a book on male objectification.

Roberta McGrath is a writer and lecturer in History and Criticism of Photography at the University of Westminster.

Sean Nixon lectures in cultural studies at the University of North London and writes on masculinity and representation. His work *Hard Looks: Masculinities, the Visual and Practices of Consumption in the 1980s* is forthcoming.

David Oswell is a lecturer in media and cultural studies at the University of Staffordshire. He is currently researching a history of children's domestic television viewing.

Kay Parkinson is doing research into HIV/AIDS and the voluntary sector at the Institute of Education in London. She has an MA in Women's Studies and is currently completing a research degree.

Naomi Salaman is an artist living in London.

Anna Marie Smith is Assistant Professor in the Department of Government at Cornell University. She is also an ACT Up activist, queer club goer and political good-time girl.

Anna Ward works for UNISON, the public service union, and is studying for an MA in Theories of Representation. She is the co-editor of *Women and Citizenship in Europe: borders, rights and duties* (Trentham, 1992).

Jeffrey Weeks is Professor of Social Relations at the University of the West of England. He is the author of numerous books on the social regulation of sexuality. These include: *Coming Out* (Quartet, 1977),

Sex, Politics and Society (Longman, 1981), *Sexuality and its Discontents* (Routledge and Kegan Paul, 1985), *Sexuality* (Tavistock, 1986), *Between the Acts* (with Kevin Porter, Routledge, 1991), and *Against Nature: Essays on History, Sexuality and Identity* (Rivers Oram Press, 1991). He is currently working on a book on sexual values.

Geoffrey Wood is Senior Examiner for the British Board of Film Classification. He is a lecturer and Director of Eastern and Central European Programmes at the Hansard Society for Parliamentary Government and has published articles on social anthropology, the teaching of the social sciences, film and pornography.